The Intentional Caregiver
Mastering Self-Care

By Geoffrey Grant

Wilmington, DE

Copyright © 2018 Geoffrey Grant. All rights reserved. No portion of this book may be reproduced mechanically, electronically, or by any other means, including photocopying, without written permission from the author. It is illegal to copy this book, post it to a website, or distribute it by any other means without permission from the author.

Author Contact: GeoffGrantConsulting.com

Thomas Noble Books

Wilmington, DE

www.thomasnoblebooks.com

Library of Congress Control Number: 2018955079

ISBN: 978-1-945586-13-2

First Printing: 2018

Editing by Gwen Hoffnagle

Cover Design by Sarah Barrie of Cyanotype.ca

All Photos Courtesy of Karen Grant

This publication is designed to provide accurate and authoritative information regarding the subject matter covered. It is sold with the understanding that the author is not engaged in rendering professional services. If legal, accounting, medical, psychological, or any other expert assistance is required, the services of a competent professional person should be sought.

DEDICATION

This book is dedicated to the memory of my parents, Faith F. and Lester J. Grant, who made me who I am;

To all those who have supported me during my caregiving journey;

And especially to Karen, with all my love, always.

Table of Contents

The Caregiver's Journey
1. The Best and Hardest Job You Never Asked For 7
2. My Caregiving Journey 15
3. Becoming an Intentional Caregiver 25
4. The Gifts of Caregiving 35

It Begins with You
5. Essential Self-Care for Caregivers 45
6. Compassion Fatigue and Burnout 57
7. Building Resilience 69
8. Setting Goals and Measuring Success 79
9. Becoming a Leader 93
10. Caregiver 911 103

Supporting Your Loved One
11. Designing and Nurturing an Alliance with Your Loved One ... 109
12. Communication Tips 119
13. Empowering Your Loved One 129
14. Asking for and Receiving Help 139
15. Forgiving Yourself and Others 149

Practicalities
16. Caregiving While Your Loved One Is at a Medical Facility ... 159
17. Logistics and Planning for Emergencies 169
18. Fostering Fun and Creativity 179
19. Finances 191
20. Intimacy and Romance 203

Summing Up
21. When Caregiving Ends 213
22. Finding and Maintaining Joy 221

About the Author 225
Acknowledgments 227

CHAPTER 1
The Best and Hardest Job You Never Asked For

The word *caregiver* first entered dictionaries in the mid-1980s, but people have been providing care to loved ones with an illness or disability for eons. Whether you are caring for a spouse, child, parent, or another, if you are a caregiver, I salute you, and I understand what you are experiencing.

I became a caregiver for my mother when I was in my thirties, about the same time that the word *caregiver* entered popular conversation. Since then I've continued in a caretaking role with my wife. I'll share my story with you soon, but I wanted to let you know from the beginning of our journey together that while others might not see the value and honor in assisting a loved one, I do.

Caregiving is full of moments of joy, hope, sorrow, and confusion. It can be physically demanding and mentally exhausting. Some of you might provide care for a short illness, while others devote decades to caring for a loved one. Some caregivers volunteer, while others become caregivers unexpectedly and perhaps reluctantly. Regardless of your situation, if you are in a caregiving role you are facing challenges that you probably did not expect. You are also in a position to make positive impacts on the life of your loved one in times of great need and great accomplishment.

The Intentional Caregiver is designed to help you not only cope with the demands of caregiving but learn to see the joy and beauty in it. You'll learn to look at your caregiving responsibilities with fresh eyes so you can choose how you want to experience caregiving and help your loved one make more intentional choices about their experiences.

There were times I felt trapped by caregiving. I struggled to care for my mother when my friends were having fun and beginning their careers, but there was no question that I would care for my mother. Both of my grandmothers lived with our family when I was a boy. In our family, taking care of elderly or ill family members was a regular part of life. When my mother had a stroke, it was up to my younger brother and me to help her. That does not mean it was easy.

This is the book I wish I had had access to then – a book full of practical ideas on making caregiving easier and more enjoyable. Most important, the information in *The Intentional Caregiver* is designed to help you grow while you are caregiving so that you become more resilient, confident, and effective in your role.

Intentional caregiving means approaching the tasks and responsibilities of helping your loved one with thoughtfulness, strength, and choice. It will give you hope and empowerment instead of your feeling constantly overwhelmed or overlooked. You'll also learn to enhance the quality of life for both your loved one and you.

Caregiving is a skill. You can learn how to do it with compassion and heart while protecting your health and energy. I've been a primary caregiver for more than twenty years, and I'm better at it today than I was at the beginning – even when I stumble or my loved one has a medical crisis. I've been burned out, angry, and frustrated as well as hopeful, reliable, and creative. Through all the ups and downs, I've learned to walk with my loved ones as they face health challenges rather than trying to control them or take away their dignity. We've worked together to figure out how to make the most of numerous medical supplies and equipment, medical appointments, and setbacks.

What I Know about You

Because you were drawn to read this book, I'm guessing you are busy with the demands of caring for a loved one. You seek support, tools, relief, and hope from someone who understands what you are experiencing. That's what you can expect from *The Intentional Caregiver*. I share everything I have learned in my journey as a caregiver as concisely and practically as possible so you can get what you need quickly and use it immediately.

You'll find questions to consider at the end of each chapter. They will help you customize the ideas to suit your style and situation. Ideally you'll use them as journaling exercises and write out your answers. Numerous research studies found that writing about your experiences and feelings helps you reduce stress, improve your immune system, and find new meaning in your experiences. (http://www.apa.org/monitor/jun02/writing.aspx)

If you decide to write out your answers to these questions, and I hope you will, you can download a free journal you can use on your computer or print and place into a notebook. You can download it at GeoffGrantConsulting.com

If you don't enjoy writing, you can think about the questions as you wait at a doctor's office, or keep them by your bedside and think about them in the middle of the night when you can't sleep. Each question is designed to help you recognize and celebrate your strengths, build resilience, and become more intentional.

QUESTIONS FOR JOURNALING

How would you describe your caregiving role today?

Did you choose to be a caregiver? Why?

Why does your loved one need your help?

What do you like the most about caregiving?

List three things, large or small, that you feel proud to provide for your loved one.

CHAPTER 2
My Caregiving Journey

When my father died in 1993, my mother vacationed during part of the winter in Florida. My younger brother and I were living in the family home in New Hampshire, both trying to figure out what we wanted to do with our lives. One day we got a phone call that changed everything.

My mother had had a massive stroke. Within hours we were on a plane to Fort Lauderdale. That's when we became caregivers, although we did not realize it at the time. My mother was left without the ability to speak and fully paralyzed on her left side. She'd been a vibrant and social person all her life, and suddenly she was without her ability to communicate, care for herself, and live independently. It was shocking.

After three months, she was well enough to make the trip back to New Hampshire to enter a rehabilitation center. While she was there, the social worker was very brusque with us, essentially saying that if we did not find a way to move my mother back home, the state would take our house and all her assets.

My brother and I went to work, remodeling the house with a wheelchair ramp and a wheelchair-accessible bathroom. After about a month, Mom was discharged, and the two of us took over her care, taking turns with twelve-hour shifts. We had no idea what we were doing and very little support. We barely knew how to cook, let alone give baths, administer medications, and keep Mom safe and healthy.

The stress was overwhelming. I felt helpless and lost. It seemed like I went from a carefree young man to an overburdened grownup overnight. Luckily my brother had a wonderful girlfriend who moved in, took over the cooking, and helped us. A few family members came to visit as well, although there was no one who lived nearby and could provide respite. Over time we found a day program and a home care agency to help, but coordinating all those services was a strain.

Then we discovered Mom had cancer, both in her breast and her lung. It was painfully hard to make decisions about her care. We tried to ask her what she wanted, but she could not tell us. We'd never really talked about end-of-life care and had no idea what kind of treatment she wanted.

In the end, we decided not to put her through more surgery and to let her cancer take its course. When we could no longer cope with her medical needs at home, we found a nursing home where she spent her last days.

After Mom died and I recovered from my grief and exhaustion, I married Karen, my long-term girlfriend, in 2001. Everything was great: I had a brand-new wife; I had a brand-new life. We were living happily ever after. Then in December of 2003, she came down with what doctors thought was pneumonia. She had an x-ray done and it showed a collapsed lung. During surgery to inflate the lung, a spot was found. Karen was twenty-nine at the time, an athlete who'd never smoked a cigarette in her life.

Her doctor sent us to Dr. David Sugarbaker at Brigham and Women's Hospital in Boston to determine why Karen had inflammation in her lungs. Dr. Sugarbaker did a thorough exam and then told us that Karen had mesothelioma in both her lungs. We had no idea what he meant or that mesothelioma was a rare cancer caused by asbestos. The doctor then told us that Karen had five months to live unless she had a very experimental surgery. He told us he did not know if the procedure would work, but it was her only option. He also said her odds of survival were less than her odds of walking on the moon.

Karen had the surgery, which was more than eight hours and very intense. Dr. Sugarbaker removed the cancer and bathed her chest in a potent chemotherapy drug. I'll never forget the terror I felt in that waiting room.

Karen spent the next five months in the hospital, primarily in ICU, and later in a rehab hospital nearby. She was on a ventilator most of that time. We communicated through gestures and writing notes. I spent every day with her, sleeping nights in her room and going home only when Dr. Sugarbaker told me I was going to fall apart if I didn't get some rest. He told me that almost every day. I'd go to the hospital every afternoon, spend the night, and be there in the morning when the doctors made their rounds.

We were blessed in many ways during that time. Dr. Sugarbaker and the staff at the hospital were very supportive. We were there so long that we got to know them very well. We still stay in touch with Dr. Sugarbaker and consider him a hero. The hospital is close to the campus of Harvard Medical School, one of the top medical institutions in the world, so she received outstanding care. Karen's family was and continues to be wonderfully supportive of us. Her parents, brothers, and relatives came to visit every day while she was in the hospital.

During those 114 days in the hospital, I got very comfortable pushing her gurney to tests and doing whatever I could to help her recover. She set a goal to go outside in her wheelchair with her ventilator at least for a few moments every day so that she could feel the sun on her face and breathe fresh air. It was a big ordeal for her and the staff, but we met that goal almost every day. When she was strong enough to be able to walk, Karen and I walked all over the hospital campus. I did my best to keep her spirits up. I purchased a portable DVD player, and we'd watch movies together. Taking care of her became the focus of my life.

Her surgery was in 2004. Thankfully Karen recovered and sits near me while I write this. She lives at home with me, although her health is fragile and she needs someone with her most of the time. I've been her caregiver since then and have learned much in the process. I'm not a saint, nor a martyr. I've grown to become a very good caregiver over time, but it has been a learning process with many ups and downs along the way.

Karen and I have a good life. We've found ways to partner so that we are both happy and fulfilled. Our relationship has deepened and become very strong. I'm honored to devote my time and energy to being her husband and caregiver. We've discovered ways to have fun, create beautiful memories, and build a life that works for us.

As you can see, I've had two very different experiences with caregiving. Both were profound experiences that taught me much about life and love. Both were challenging, painful at times, with periods of stress, overwhelm, and burnout. I've found new strength and confidence because of the challenges I've faced, and become a much more compassionate person.

And yet there are days when I get cranky, tired, or feel sorry for myself. Karen and I get into disagreements like any other married couple. Life can be messy and challenging sometimes. We've had tussles with insurance companies, doctors, and the medical establishment. We live in Massachusetts where there are long winters and power outages that require us to relocate to a place with electricity for her ventilator. Our life is not easy or perfect, but it's real, and we are thankful for each day we have together.

One of the most significant gifts in my caregiving journey has been the opportunity for personal development. I've learned many lessons and am proud to be able to share them with you in this book.

QUESTIONS FOR JOURNALING

What are some of your most cherished moments spent in the hospital or other medical facility with your loved one?

Were there moments when you lost hope or felt afraid during your loved one's stay at the medical facility? How might you handle such emotions more effectively in the future?

What did you do to stay healthy during long periods waiting by your loved one's bedside?

My Caregiving Journey

What did a medical professional do to give you hope or outstanding care?

After reading about my journey, how would you now describe your caregiving as a journey beyond the role you described in the chapter 1 question?

CHAPTER 3
Becoming an Intentional Caregiver

The *Merriam-Webster Dictionary* defines the word *intentional* as something done by design, with the end in mind. This might seem like a strange word to use regarding caregiving, which is often unexpected and unplanned. We rarely know when our loved ones will experience a health crisis. Part of the stress involved in caregiving is that it can come up suddenly, and we don't have time to mentally or physically prepare for it.

When Karen was diagnosed with lung cancer at age twenty-nine, we were shocked, as she had never smoked and always took care of her health. Your loved one's health crisis likely arrived suddenly, too. It may not have been your intention or plan to become a caregiver, but you rose to the challenge and are probably doing things you never expected to do. That shows courage. I salute you!

> **An intentional caregiver is one who cares for a loved one with thoughtfulness and a commitment to honoring the dignity and strengths of both the loved one and the caregiver.**

I believe that it is possible to be an intentional caregiver even in an unexpected situation. Being intentional about caregiving has given me strength and comfort and has enhanced my ability to work with Karen on her health and quality of life.

This concept came to me gradually. In the early days of caring for my wife, I approached caregiving as a set of tasks, similar to how I approached my mother's care. I focused on getting things done – administering medications, attending medical appointments, and working with insurance and community agencies. It was a lot of work, and my mind was continually focused on getting the next thing done. I did not have the time or capacity to think deeply about my feelings or even about ways I could partner with Karen to make her experience more fulfilling. When I was stressed or tired, I just told myself to suck it up and keep going. Perhaps this is your experience, too.

Things started to shift for me when I attended a caregiver support group and learned that I could choose how I wanted to feel about my role as a caregiver. I'd never heard of such an idea, and it opened up new possibilities for me. Since then I've spent much time and thought, as well as research and work with other caregivers, on the idea of approaching caregiving with intention.

Shifting your mindset to intentional caregiving decreases your stress and empowers you to work more effectively with your loved one, other family members, and the medical community. You will still have tasks to complete, but approaching them with an intentional mindset helps you manage all the tasks and demands more easily.

To become an intentional caregiver, consider these ideas:

- **You are not a victim.** This is very important. You have decided to provide care for your loved one and can be proud of that decision.
- **Your feelings matter and you are in control of them.** Feelings are neither right nor wrong, they just are. Some days you will feel angry, worried, delighted, or hopeful. Our society has taught us that some feelings are wrong and should be avoided. That's not true. So-called negative emotions such as fear and anger can provide the energy to take action. When you feel an emotion that is not pleasant for you, you can decide if you want to stay stuck in that emotion or do something to shift it.

  Both caregivers and their loved ones often hide their emotions. You don't want to burden your loved one with your feelings, and they don't want to burden you either. Instead of hiding feelings, try having a gentle discussion about how your loved one is doing and why they feel that way. Don't be afraid when your loved one feels strong emotions. Just listen. You can open the conversation with some easy questions like:
    o How do you feel about all this?
    o What do you think about starting physical therapy tomorrow?

- Are you concerned about going home next week?
- You seem sad today day. Would you like to talk about it?

And when you are feeling powerful emotions, you can share them honestly with your loved one without putting them in the position of your therapist, especially if they are medically fragile. Honestly sharing your feelings is respectful and honors their place in your life, even if you say something as simple as "I'm having a rough day today because I am worried about your test results." When you share your feelings with your loved one, you are also encouraging them to share their feelings and not pretend that everything is okay when they are in pain.

- **Actions can help shift emotions.** We all have days when we feel angry or depressed, even when we're healthy. When you or your loved one are experiencing a down day, the intentional approach is to notice and name the emotion, then figure out a way to feel better. You don't have to wait for something outside you to fix the situation; you can act – and that always feels more empowering.

  The intentional caregiver might say:
  - I'm feeling isolated and bored today. What can I do to make today more fun for me and my loved one?
  - My loved one is sad and depressed about their prognosis. How can I honor those emotions and still keep my hope alive?
  - My loved one is back in the hospital for another surgery. I'm so worried. What can I do to relax while I'm waiting?

- **Your role as a caregiver is important.** Medical personnel might not always show you the respect you deserve. Have you had an experience in which someone referred to you as "the husband," "the mother," "the sister," or another term that made you feel more like a thing than a person? Unfortunately this happens frequently. I say something like this in those situations: "Hi, I'm Geoff, Karen's husband and her primary caregiver. I am looking forward to working with you."

- **You and your loved one can form a powerful alliance that supports both of you.** I need to help Karen with bathing. The first few times, we were both uncomfortable. I finally asked her how she'd like me to help her and what we could do to make the process feel better. We experimented and found the most comfortable techniques for both of us, which included some jokes and light-hearted conversation to break the tension. Having that conversation made all the difference.

  You'll read much more later in the book about forming an alliance with your loved one; for now just consider that it is possible for you and your loved one to work together to enrich your day-to-day lives, even when your loved one is medically fragile or cannot communicate.

- **An intentional caregiver views their loved one holistically.** This means that you don't just focus on the minutia of providing medical and personal care but stand as an advocate for increasing the self-respect, independence, and quality of life for your loved one, whether they are in the hospital, a care center, or at home. The medical community focuses on just the body.

As the caregiver, you can look deeper and find ways to honor all of your loved one – body, mind, and spirit.

Do this by asking yourself what you can do to improve the life of your loved one. Doing little things to make them smile can be deeply rewarding. When Karen was in the hospital all those months after her lung surgery, I once brought her pet rabbits to the hospital just to cheer her up. I was proud that I could do something that brightened her day in the midst of her pain. That moment was just as important as the practical things I did. All it took was thoughtfulness.

If I had to sum up the idea of becoming an intentional caregiver, I'd say that intentional caregivers employ a thoughtful approach to caregiving that honors the needs, strengths, and wishes of both the loved one and the caregiver. That might be a new idea for you. It certainly was for me. When I began to look at my caregiving this way, it was very helpful for me and Karen. It will enhance your experience, too.

Developing this intentional mindset is a process that requires some time. It doesn't have to be hard or arduous. Instead, caregiving with intention is a way of thinking that empowers both you and your loved one.

QUESTIONS FOR JOURNALING

How do you feel about the idea of approaching your caregiving with intention?

What makes you proud about the care you have provided thus far?

If you have been disrespected or overlooked by a medical professional, how might you handle such a situation in the future?

The Intentional Caregiver

What emotions have you been afraid to share with your loved one?

What ideas do you have today about enhancing your loved one's quality of life?

CHAPTER 4
The Gifts of Caregiving

No one is going to give you a corner office, a gold medal, or a raise in salary for your caregiving efforts. The gifts of caregiving are like hidden treasures that wait quietly to be discovered in the midst of the experience. There are many gifts, but you will find them only in retrospect when you look back over your day or your month and notice how you've grown or remember special moments.

One of the subtle gifts of caregiving is developing courage. You'll often be scared in your caregiving journey, and so will your loved one. You'll be frightened of making mistakes, of what the future holds, of another long day watching your loved one endure another painful treatment. It can be scary the first time you have to give an injection, hook up a ventilator, or try to get your loved one from a wheelchair into the car for the first time. Over time you'll realize that you've developed the capacity to be scared and keep moving forward anyway. That's courage, and caregiving will certainly give you that gift. You'll also witness the courage of your loved one as they fight to breathe or regain strength.

Karen's known me for a long time. She saw me taking care of my mother and helped me at times. One of my happiest memories is the day when Karen and I got my mom in the car and took her out to eat. Mom loved lobster rolls, and when she got to have one at a favorite restaurant, her eyes were shining. At that moment I knew we'd found a way to give Mom a moment of happiness. I'll cherish that memory for the rest of my life.

You can't give your loved one a cure or restore all they've lost, but you can provide moments that are more precious than anything else. That's another gift of caregiving: the wisdom that life is all about the moments. When you intentionally create moments of joy, peace, comfort, or laugher for your loved one, you enjoy them, too. Those moments you share make the work and sacrifice of caregiving worthwhile.

People often tell me that I'm wise. I smile because I used to be a young man with a sick mom who didn't know how to cope or what to do next. I think the reason I seem wise today is that caregiving's taught me what matters: moments of connection, commitment, love, and doing the right thing even when it's hard. It's also shown me what doesn't matter. I don't have career success, a fancy car, or a lavish lifestyle. Those don't matter to me at all. I have Karen, and she's alive. What more could I want?

Early on, when Karen was in the hospital, she told me that I could divorce her and she would not blame me. She'd seen me struggle to care for Mom and did not want to put me through a similar experience. One of the nurses told me that at least fifty percent of marriages end when one of the partners gets cancer. I could have left Karen and walked away. She gave me permission, which shows you what a beautiful person she is. I can still see us in her hospital room that day. I said, "Of course not. I'm here with you for whatever it takes. We are going to fight this together. You would do the same for me."

Being her caregiver has shown me what real love is. We have worked hard together to develop an alliance that gives us joy and happiness. When you care for your loved one, you love them in the most sacred and profound way possible. You love them through their best and worst moments. They might not be able to thank you with words, but they know and sincerely appreciate all your efforts. When you are family, you care for each other in good times and bad. You can feel a sense of pride in demonstrating your love and commitment every day of your caregiving journey. It's noble and honorable. That feeling of satisfaction for keeping your promise to love and care will sustain you.

Caregiving has given me the gift of empathy and compassion for my loved one and for others. I was an ordinary young man, not particularly aware of empathy and compassion before my mom had her stroke. My focus was on figuring out my adult life and having fun. All the time I've spent in hospitals has helped me develop deep compassion for others and myself. There is no way to be a perfect caregiver. I've failed as many times as I've done well. I've had to learn to forgive myself and be compassionate to myself. That's helped me be more understanding when Karen's having a bad day, when a medical professional is curt and unfeeling, or when the insurance representative won't give me answers.

I've also become able to laugh and try again. Sometimes I blow it. The adage "If at first you don't succeed, try, try again" rings true for caregivers. I've learned that I can learn. That might sound silly, but it is possible to learn how to tackle all the tasks of caregiving. I've learned that if I fail the first time, I can ask for help and keep trying until I can do it. It helps to laugh.

One of the most significant gifts I've received from being a caregiver is to love and care for myself. This took a long time. At first my focus was solely on my loved one. I believed I could power through their illness and ignore myself. I mistakenly thought that the more I sacrificed my health and well-being, the better it would be for my loved one.

Over time and with the help of a support group, a therapist, and a life coach, I learned the importance of filling my bucket with whatever energy I need so I can give my best to Karen. Filling my bucket means that I recognize and honor my own needs as well as Karen's. When I began to pay attention to my mind, body, and spirit, I did a better job with my caregiving tasks. I could laugh more, be more creative, and respond with more compassion. I had to learn to love myself through my best and worst moments, which was harder for me than loving Karen at her best and worst. Loving yourself is a challenge, especially during times of high stress; yet it is an essential part of successful caregiving. I've provided care when I loved myself and when I hated and ignored myself; it is much easier when I'm treating myself with love and compassion.

What about You?

In a perfect world, you would have read this book before you started your caregiving journey. But you probably came to this book as a caregiver – perhaps tired, worried, and depleted. It might seem ludicrous to even consider that caregiving can give you gifts, but now that you've read about some of the gifts that I've gleaned from providing care, I hope that you'll be able to look for the quietly hidden treasures that you've earned.

My hope is that this idea will sink into your awareness; that over time you'll start to notice how you are growing in confidence, courage, compassion, and the ability to love and care for yourself so that you can care for your loved one. It is a process that takes time and reflection. Even on busy and stressful days, you can spend a moment before you go to sleep or while you are folding laundry and ask yourself questions like these:

- What went well today?
- How am I improving?
- What moments do I want to remember?
- In what ways did I demonstrate courage or compassion today?
- What did I do to fill my own bucket?

Reflecting on your experience every day helps you notice the happy moments and your growth. This reflection doesn't have to take much time or effort, and it is a beneficial habit to develop.

Many caregivers find that writing in a journal is a good way to consider these questions. If you don't enjoy journaling, identify a mindless task that you do every day and plan to reflect on these questions while you are doing that task so that reflection becomes a healthy habit. Perhaps you can think about these things when you are brushing your teeth or showering. Most caregivers find time to do that almost every day!

QUESTIONS FOR JOURNALING

What gifts has caregiving given you?

How have you grown in confidence and courage?

Can you recall a time you had to forgive yourself and try again with a caregiving task? Write about what you learned from that.

The Intentional Caregiver

What simple steps can you take today to fill your own bucket?

How do you define compassion? Can you offer it to yourself as well as to others?

CHAPTER 5

Essential Self-Care for Caregivers

When you are a caregiver, many people tell you to rest and take care of yourself. They mean well, but sometimes those comments can make you even more tired. I remember thinking, "Yeah, right. I'm just going to head off to the beach and leave all my caregiving responsibilities behind." You already know that you need to watch your health by getting enough sleep, some exercise, and eating healthy meals on a regular schedule. It can be challenging to do this, especially if your loved one is in the hospital or in a fragile state at home.

In this chapter, I'm not just going to tell you to get more rest, but give you concrete strategies for taking care of yourself so you have the energy and capacity to care for your loved one.

Create Allies and Communicate Often

It takes a team to provide care and support the caregiver. One of the most important things you can do is create allies – people who will help you with some aspects of caregiving. Look to your family members, friends, neighbors, people who attend your religious organization, and community agencies. Many people will offer to help saying, "Call me if I can do anything." Take them up on that offer!

There are many ways people can help, even if they live far away. Here's a list to start you thinking about practical ways people can support you:

- Managing finances and dealing with insurance companies – excellent tasks for someone who lives out of town or cannot provide physical care
- Grocery shopping
- Home modifications or cleaning
- Visiting with your loved one while you go out for a meal, haircut, or just to take a break
- Picking up medications or supplies
- Preparing the house for a return from the hospital: stocking up on towels and medical supplies/equipment; comfortable, easy-to-don clothing; food; and paper goods
- Bringing in meals
- Coordinating volunteers who come in regularly to help in long-term situations, such as when a child needs supervision doing their physical therapy exercises
- Taking your loved one on outings or helping them do hobbies at home
- Visiting with your loved one regularly by phone, email, or letter
- Staying overnight with your loved one so you can rest or travel

While your loved one is in the hospital or rehab center, ask their social worker for referrals for appropriate community services such as respite care, home health, and day programs. Learn about any federal or state assistance available for help. Some insurance policies have a provision for home health care, so check with your insurer.

It might seem like a lot of work to create these allies and communicate with them often. It is worth it! Every moment you spend building a team of partners to help you translates into a moment when you can rest and when your loved one can see a new face. Lessening isolation for both of you is a very healthy practice.

Organization

When you are a caregiver, you can become extremely stressed, especially when your loved one is in a health crisis. It's hard to think clearly. As soon as you possibly can, take some time to organize things so you don't have to worry about them so much. Consider these things:

- Does your loved one have a will, power of attorney, and advanced directive? If not, get those documents taken care of.
- Gather all that paperwork – driver's license or identification card, insurance cards, list of prescriptions, names of all treating physicians, and medical history – and place it in a brightly colored folder for easy access.
- Review your loved one's financial situation. This task is of course easier when caring for a spouse or child. If it is your parent who is ill, enlist one of your siblings,

- if possible, to find and organize your parent's finances and share that information with all your siblings.
- When possible, talk with your loved one about their wishes for medical treatment and care options. If your loved one cannot communicate, have discussions with family members to reach a consensus about care options and quality of life.
- When your loved one is at home, create a schedule or easy way to track appointments, medication administration, and medical treatments so that you don't have to keep that information in your head.
- Create a routine that works for both of you. For example, you might rest in the mornings and visit your loved one in the hospital in the afternoons. Establish a specific time of day when you can read, walk around the block, or do something just for yourself. Routines reduce stress for caregivers and loved ones.

Create Personal Goals

When you are a caregiver, you can't measure your efforts easily. Your loved one may have a health setback or even pass away – that does not mean that you have failed. You cannot control their health, although you can do much to contribute to their healing process. Consider how you want to approach caregiving and your well-being. Create simple goals, write them down, and feel the satisfaction and accomplishment of checking them off your list, such as:

- Organizing all the insurance paperwork
- Setting up home delivery of medications and groceries

- Finding someone to cover your responsibilities while you go to the gym or exercise at home three times each week
- Encouraging your loved one to smile or laugh every day
- Finding a way to get at least seven hours of sleep each night
- Putting a bird feeder up near the bedroom window and keeping it filled with seed
- Attending an online support group weekly

Personal goals can be one-time tasks, things you regularly do, or even embracing how you want to feel about caregiving tasks. This is such an essential topic for the intentional caregiver that I devote all of chapter 8 to exploring it more deeply. For today, just start to think about personal goals that will enhance your caregiving journey.

Discuss Your Well-Being with Your Loved One

As soon as possible, start to talk about your well-being with your loved one. Plant seeds early that you are paying attention to your health so that you can have the stamina to care for them. Many people feel guilty when they need help, and your loved one might be worrying about you as much as you are concerned about them. Put their mind at ease. Use phrases like:

- I'm going to get a good dinner and then some sleep so I can come back to see you early tomorrow when the doctor makes rounds.
- I'm feeling really tired, so I'm going to get a little fresh air.
- The hospital has a support group for family members. I'm going to attend so that I can learn how to best take care of you at home.

- I'm going out to dinner with Joe, and Mary is going to come over and stay with you. I need a little mental break.
- I want to be strong and healthy for you, so I'm going to start exercising every day.

Be aware that these conversations may sting your loved a little bit or even make them fearful, especially if you have been their only caregiver for a long time. They might feel sad that you want time away from them or feel worried that someone who is coming in to help might not be able to meet their needs. That is why it is so important to start talking about your well-being as soon as possible instead of waiting until you are falling apart and then surprising your loved one with the topic.

Remember that you cannot give to your loved one if your bucket is empty. If you develop *compassion fatigue* or burnout, you won't have the strength, clarity of mind, or emotional capacity to do all that your loved one needs. (I discuss compassion fatigue and burnout in the next chapter.)

Respite Care

Karen and I are blessed. Her parents and siblings live nearby and are always willing to help us. At one point in the ten years that I've been her caregiver, I was even able to get a full-time job because she was doing very well medically, and her family stepped in to meet her needs while I was at work. Even though my work situation changed and it was no longer practical for me to work outside our home, Karen's family still steps in regularly to provide me with time away.

After eight years of caring for Karen at home, I went on a retreat for a couple of days. This time of respite was invaluable for me, refreshing me mentally, spiritually, emotionally, and physically. Now I plan two short trips each year to work on myself.

Respite care is the term used by insurance companies and healthcare providers for temporary care provided by someone other than the primary caregiver. Karen does not qualify for respite care under her insurance coverage because her health is improving. We have to budget for respite care and always appreciate the support we get from her family. They are the best!

Respite is just a fancy word for taking a break from your responsibilities as a caregiver. It can be as simple as time to attend a class or support group each week, or as complicated as taking a week-long trip. Respite requires planning and working together with your loved one to find solutions that work well for both of you. I suggest starting slowly with something simple that does not require much time away from home. In that way, you, your loved one, and the respite provider build your confidence.

Some insurance policies cover regular respite care or in-home services. If your loved one has an in-home aide, start by going on a short trip for coffee with a friend or even just running errands to see how things go while you are gone. Talk with the provider and your loved one about how things went. Always monitor the situation to ensure that things are going correctly and that your loved one feels safe and comfortable.

If a friend or family member will be providing the respite care, train them before the respite care begins. Orient them to what needs to be done, where things are located, what to do in an emergency, and any specific signs they need to watch for that signal a change in medical status. Leave a list of phone numbers and be readily available by phone.

Once you and your loved one have had a few short respite experiences, you can build up slowly to longer times away. Use your good judgment here and work in partnership with your loved one. Be ready to change your plans or schedule if a health crisis arises.

You can choose to do anything you like during your times of respite. I enjoy doing things that enhance my well-being, so I attend groups or classes, exercise, take in a movie, or attend an event with a friend or relative. When I am going out of town, it is for a retreat or learning opportunity.

It is vital that you share your plans with your loved one before you go so they don't feel like you are making plans behind their back to get away from them. They might enjoy hearing about a movie, ball game, or concert. Being aware of their feelings and openly communicating ensures that you and your loved one come to view times of respite as part of your routine.

QUESTIONS FOR JOURNALING

When you read the list of ways that others can support your caregiving efforts, how did you feel?

Who can help you?

What steps have you already taken to organize your time and the tasks of caregiving?

How would you rate your well-being at this point? What changes are you inspired to start making now?

If you suddenly had one hour's respite each week, what would you enjoy doing first?

CHAPTER 6

Compassion Fatigue and Burnout

In the 1980s, researchers began to notice a set of symptoms common to people in caregiving roles that they termed *compassion fatigue*. Initial research focused on medical professionals and first responders to traumatic events. Over time researchers realized that compassion fatigue could severely impact family caregivers as well, sometimes more deeply because of the love they have for their ill family members.

The American Institute of Stress defines *compassion fatigue* as "the emotional residue or strain of exposure to working with those suffering from the consequences of traumatic events." *Burnout* is defined as a "cumulative process marked by emotional exhaustion and withdrawal associated with increased workload and stress." (https://www.stress.org/military/for-practitionersleaders/compassion-fatigue)

Researchers writing in the *International Journal of Environmental and Public Health* looked at all the literature on compassion fatique and developed this definition: "Compassion Fatique is characterized by exhaustion, anger and irritability, negative coping behaviours including alcohol and drug abuse, reduced ability to feel sympathy and empathy, a diminished sense of enjoyment or satisfaction with work, increased absenteeism, and an impaired ability to make decisions and care for patients." (https://www.ncbi.nlm.nih.gov/pmc/articles/PMC4924075)

In my experience, the symptoms of compassion fatigue and burnout come on subtly and slowly. It's difficult to notice that you are starting to feel overwhelmed, exhausted, and down, especially if you haven't heard much about these terms before. As you review the material in this chapter, notice if you are experiencing any of the symptoms. Don't worry if you are. These challenges are common for all caregivers. I don't want to frighten you, just educate you and provide some simple ways you can start to feel better.

Caregivers experience both compassion fatigue and burnout because they witness traumatic events such as surgeries and heart attacks, and they have a constant workload of caregiving tasks. These are some of the common symptoms:

- Mental, physical, and emotional exhaustion
- Apathy, sadness, and anger
- Difficulty concentrating, sleeping, and making decisions
- Feeling trapped or victimized
- Working on autopilot without feeling anything
- Masking pain with alcohol, drugs, food, shopping, or other distractions

- Neglecting your appearance, health, and/or self-care
- Chronic health issues such as headaches, colds, and stomach problems
- Loss of self-esteem, efficiency, and/or effectiveness

Compassion fatigue and burnout are dangerous for both the caregiver and their loved one. An exhausted caregiver is more apt to make mistakes with medications or miss appointments. Unchecked, compassion fatigue and burnout can lead to severe depression and prevent the caregiver from helping their loved one at all.

When I was caregiving for my mother, I suffered from compassion fatigue and burnout, although I didn't realize it at the time. My stress began when I was told that I had no choice but to take care of my mother or all her financial assets would be stripped away. I felt threatened, and that feeling was like a sword over my head waiting to drop at any moment. I was happy to take care of my mother, but the idea that I was being forced to do it with that kind of a threat set the stage for profound worry and emotional pain. This experience told me that my feelings did not matter, that I had no choice, and that I'd be punished unless I did what I was told. These were not helpful thoughts in a stressful and traumatic situation.

Before her stroke, my mother was a big part of my life. We loved talking and laughing together. When she became ill, I was grieving the loss of her friendship and support, but I had no time to think about my feelings, only to figure out how to cope with her needs. My mother never recovered. We had no hope that she would ever improve, which was terribly painful.

I dealt with that pain by drinking too much and neglecting my health.

One moment stands out clearly. I traveled to Florida to sell Mom's condo while my brother took care of her. I was on a beautiful beach but could not enjoy the ocean, only worry about Mom and feel guilty about not being with her to make sure she was okay.

After Mom's cancer diagnosis, my brother and I decided we had to admit her to a nursing home. We drove to where she was to be admitted but when we got there we turned the car around and went back home. We just could not do it. In the end, we looked at countless places before we found one we liked. We were both so burned out and emotionally exhausted that it was a relief to admit her to the nursing home at that point.

My experience in caring for Karen has been different. I'm wiser now and more aware of the importance of taking care of myself. Early on I noticed that I was starting to feel burned out, so I began to work on myself. I felt melancholy and like a victim, which drained my power to act effectively. I joined a caregiving support group and started to work with a life coach. One day I learned that I could choose how I wanted to feel. This opened up a new world for me. Before that I hadn't paid a lot of attention to my feelings. I was focused on getting things done and making sure Karen had all she needed. Focusing on my choices helped me feel empowered. The situation had not changed, but I started seeing it in a new way and enjoying the fact that I had chosen to be Karen's caregiver and was pretty good at it. That's the day I became an intentional caregiver.

Today I am very intentional about maintaining my health and well-being. I realize that it's my responsibility to stay healthy so that I can give Karen what she needs. I want us both to be as happy and healthy as possible, so I pay attention to my state of mind. I'm committed to being healthy so that I can both take care of her and enjoy life.

Victims, Martyrs, and Superheroes

It can be easy for caregivers to slip into the thought pattern of a victim, a martyr, or a superhero. When you feel like a victim, you focus on how trapped you are and that you don't have any choices in your life. A martyr wants credit or praise for sacrificing everything for their loved one. A superhero believes that they are the only one who can provide care for their loved one and require no help or rest. I've had all of these thought patterns at one time or another, and you might as well.

These thought patterns come from stress, tiredness, and worry. They can sneak up on you, and before you know it you're stuck in a pattern that makes you feel weaker and more tired. When you're thinking this way, it's hard to give your loved one the support required.

The best antidote for unhealthy thought patterns is to remind yourself that you always have a choice. You are doing noble work in caring for your loved one, and no one is holding a gun to your head to force you to do it. It is a beautiful and honorable choice. It also gives you rewards such as feelings of satisfaction, deepened relationships, and precious memories. You are both giving and receiving.

Compassion Fatigue and Burnout Prevention

You can combat compassion fatigue and burnout, or heal from them, by making some new choices in your daily routine and remembering to notice the state of your well-being. Dr. Figley shared a list of ideas for preventing compassion fatigue and burnout in the Compassion Fatigue Educator (CFE) certification program offered through The Figley Institute and the Green Cross Academy of Traumatology.

Here are some of my favorites:

Cognitive:

- Make lists.
- Break big decisions and tasks into smaller steps.
- Make small choices every day.
- Research and learn as much as possible before making a large decision.
- Set small and large goals; have a plan for your future.
- Realize you always have options.
- Remember the times you were successful and made wise decisions.

Behavioral:

- Try new things and revisit past hobbies.
- Relax.
- Ask for help.
- Spend time alone and with others.
- Explore new ideas and places – even a simple visit to a new store or restaurant.
- Do things in moderation.

Emotional:

- Allow yourself to experience your feelings; label them.
- Have a buddy you can vent with.
- Use humor and watch funny movies.
- Be assertive when needed.
- Make communication a priority.
- Use positive language when possible, with yourself and others.

Spiritual:

- Practice your faith or spiritual rituals.
- Read empowering and uplifting books.
- Pray.
- Meditate or practice mindfulness.
- Connect with a faith group or spiritual advisor.
- Celebrate the beauty of creation.

Interpersonal:

- Give and receive hugs.
- Set appropriate boundaries.
- Spend time with friends and loved ones.
- State your needs clearly.
- Apologize when needed.
- Play and laugh together.

Physical:

- Eat sensibly, including healthy food and regular meals.
- Drink water.

- Get enough sleep.
- Continue to see your own doctor and dentist.
- Exercise regularly.
- Breathe deeply.
- Wear comfortable clothing and shoes.
- Enjoy a warm bath or regular massage.

http://www.figleyinstitute.com/documents/Workbook_AMEDD_SanAntonio_2012July20_RevAugust2013.pdf

These can seem like positive suggestions or just more weight on your shoulders. If you feel stressed just reading this list, you will benefit from committing more time to your well-being. (The "Practicalities" section provides even more suggestions about caregiver self-care.)

QUESTIONS FOR JOURNALING

How does this information about compassion fatigue and burnout impact you?

What are you currently doing to support yourself?

What warning signs of compassion fatigue or burnout do you notice in yourself?

Which preventative behaviors in the list above might you be able to start on right now?

Do you have enough support? If not, who might you ask for help?

CHAPTER 7
Building Resilience

We had a severe winter in the northeast this year. There were blizzards with power outages, heaps of snow, and bitter temperatures. While winter is challenging for many, it can be a serious problem for Karen and me. She needs electricity for her medical equipment. Without that equipment, she can't use the ventilator.

The first time we lost our electricity after Karen came home from the hospital, I went into a panic. Now I watch the weather and make reservations at a hotel before a storm hits. I have a list of hotels with handicapped-accessible rooms, on-site restaurants, and backup generators. It's a hassle and an unexpected expense, but nothing that we can't manage.

When I look back over my caregiving journey, I'm surprised by how I've grown in confidence and resilience. Resilience is the capacity to recover quickly from difficulties. It's an unexpected gift given to caregivers over time. Consider it your bonus.

If you are already caregiving, you probably remember the initial fear, worry, stress, and anxiety of the first days. I recall an experience in the grocery store when I just couldn't cope with my caregiving responsibilities. I thought I was having a heart attack because my heart was pounding and I felt dizzy. The stress of my situation was overwhelming me. You may have had a similar experience.

When you are a caregiver, you'll be asked to do many new things. The first time you give an injection, help transfer your loved one from the bed to a wheelchair, or assist with bathing, you'll be scared. You won't know how to do things and you'll worry about honoring the dignity of your loved one. There will be many first times in your caregiving journey, and all of them can be stressful.

The good news is that each time you do something for the first time, you gain confidence and resilience. You'll remember the best techniques and how to approach your loved one in a way that works for both of you. There is a saying, "You never know how strong you are until being strong is the only option." You become resilient over time by facing challenges and solving problems.

You'll also experience things that don't go well. When I first started providing care for my mother, some caregiving tasks seemed easy while others were very challenging. Changing her diapers was stressful, especially during the night when I was exhausted from the day's tasks. My brother took on the job of the overnight changing, which was a real blessing. This experience taught me to accept without guilt that I could fail or need help to complete some of the requirements of caregiving. Failing is learning in disguise, and a builder of resilience.

One of the best ways to develop resilience is to focus on your strengths and acknowledge your growth over time. When I was my mother's caregiver, I discovered that I have a talent for logistics. I'm lucky that way. When there is a problem to be solved, something in me rises to the occasion and I create a plan. The plan might not be perfect and often needs some adjusting, but managing logistics helps me feel confident and resilient. I know that everything will work out.

Maybe you don't have a talent for logistics but you are able to coax a laugh from your loved one, prepare nourishing meals, give a soothing backrub, or negotiate with insurance companies. Every caregiver has personal strengths and develops more of them over time. Caregiving is never easy, but developing resilience helps you cope more effectively with caregiving challenges.

The American Psychological Association offers these suggestions for developing resilience:

- Connect with others.
- Focus on a positive future instead of the immediate crisis.
- Set goals and work towards them.
- Accept that change is part of life.
- Take decisive action.
- Maintain hope.
- Write about or discuss your feelings.
- Connect with meaningful spiritual practices.
- Recognize how the challenge helps you grow.

(http://www.apa.org/helpcenter/road-resilience.aspx)

Another way to build your resilience is to remember the reciprocity of your relationship. When I would get stressed or tired, I'd imagine what would have happened if I had been the one with the illness. Karen and my mother would have done everything in their power to care for me. Remembering what they have done for me in other areas of my life helped me refresh my energy for caregiving.

Consider what gifts your loved one has given you. Remember the happy moments, the times when they lifted you up, and the things you faced together. Draw on those memories and moments to build your resilience.

When you think about it, you have a choice to continue as a caregiver or not. Each day brings you the opportunity to love and protect your family member. You've made that choice every day of your caregiving journey, most likely because of your love and commitment. Remembering all the days you chose to be a caregiver strengthens your resilience.

Resilience grows over time. You can't get it from reading a book, but understanding how it builds on itself enables you to see that you are becoming stronger and more confident. Since writing about your experience is a way to increase your resilience, I provided extra journaling questions in this chapter. Even if you don't usually write out your answers to the questions, I invite you to do so with these as a resilience exercise. You will discover important things about yourself.

QUESTIONS FOR JOURNALING

What skills have you mastered since becoming a caregiver?

What was the most challenging thing you did for your loved one?

How do you hold on to hope regardless of your loved one's mood or prognosis?

Do you consider yourself resilient? Why or why not?

Remember the day before your loved one grew ill. How are you stronger now?

Why do you care for your loved one?

What has your loved one given you?

If you have a spiritual practice, how does it support you?

List the reasons you are proud of your caregiving journey.

CHAPTER 8
Setting Goals and Measuring Success

Caregiving happens out of the public eye. You are rarely seen or acknowledged for your efforts. While most of us will be caregivers at some point in our lives, few consider caregiving a career or personal goal. It's a role you assume, not aspire to. Caregiving tasks are not glamorous. Who gets excited about helping with toileting or tooth brushing?

There is an old saying that applies to what you are being called to do: "God's work for God's pay." Many caregivers don't expect any rewards or acknowledgment for their actions; they just want their loved one to be safe, comfortable, and healthy. In fact, it can be uncomfortable when someone praises us for our caregiving. I remember Karen's surgeon telling me that I contributed to her good health. I was embarrassed and could not accept that compliment for a long time because I didn't value what I did.

And yet caregiving is extremely valuable. Consider what might happen to your loved one if you were not around. While no one will give you an award or a trophy, you are truly helping your loved one endure vulnerable and painful moments. It is a sacred and honorable act, and certainly one of deep love and commitment.

Defining a Successful Caregiver

Early in my caregiving experience, I thought that if Mom had a good day or showed signs of recovery, I was doing a good job. However, that viewpoint did not serve me well when my mother died. I wondered if her death made me a failure because I could not heal her. I even felt guilty for feeling relieved that she was no longer suffering.

It is essential to separate your loved one's medical condition from how you value your caregiving. Your loved one might decline, face new medical challenges, or pass away. That is not something you can control. Let me be very clear: If your loved one has a setback or passes way, you have not failed. If you get tired, make a mistake, or have an argument, you are not a lousy caregiver, you are a human being.

It can be easy to set up unrealistic expectations such as being sweet, supportive, and loving at all times; never missing an appointment; and going for days without sleep so that your loved one is not alone in the hospital. The good news is that you don't have to be perfect or superhuman to be a good caregiver. Focus on what you can control, which is *your* behavior, health, and attitude.

My definition of a successful caregiver is someone who approaches caregiving with intention, dedication, love, and compassion while keeping themselves healthy. Your definition might be different. Each caregiver decides for themselves what constitutes success. It might be as simple as getting through each day with your sense of humor and sanity intact, or as complex as a list of written goals.

The Value of Personal Goals

Because you don't have a supervisor who will give you a performance evaluation, it can be helpful to create some short- and long-term goals. With this measuring stick, you'll know if you've achieved what you would like to or need to try again tomorrow. Goals give you focus and direction.

You might have heard about S.M.A.R.T. goals, which is a term frequently used in business and personal-development settings:

S – specific: This means that you can see whether or not the goal was achieved. You can't see something like a good attitude, but you can see whether or not you ate a green vegetable.

M – measurable: The most valuable goals include a number by which to measure them.

A – achievable: This element is the most challenging for caregivers. Since the health of your loved one can change quickly, what seems achievable at the beginning of a week can be unrealistic by the end of that week. I recommend small goals that don't add pressure but keep you moving towards the ideal.

R – relevant: Does the goal make sense in the context of your life? If you are a caregiver, a goal to climb Mount Everest is probably not relevant (unless it is related to a dream you share with your loved one).

T – time-bound: How long will you work on this goal, or how long can you expect it to take to achieve it?

Compare these two goals:
1. I'm going to lose weight.
2. I will lose ten pounds in the next ninety days.

The second goal can be easily measured. At the end of ninety days, the scale will reveal whether or not the goal was reached. It includes the components of a SMART goal.

When considering goals for caregiving, you can't set goals for your loved one such as "Dad will be walking by Christmas," but you can set goals for yourself and how you approach caregiving. A SMART goal for a caregiver might be "This week I'm going to go to the gym on Monday and Thursday afternoon and talk with Dad about how good it feels to exercise."

Short-term goals take a week or a month, while long-term goals take longer. For example, Karen and I have a goal to go on a vacation together next year. She has not been able to travel for many years, so this goal has many steps for us to complete together as well as things I need to do. A short-term goal might be to research over the next week five hotels in the area we wish to travel to.

I invite you to create some long- and short-term goals for each topic below and record them in your journal. A goal that is written down has more power – you are more likely to take it seriously. I use Post-it® notes to record my weekly goals, and keep a list of my long-term goals in my journal.

Have fun creating these goals. Share them with your loved one. Encourage them to set goals as well so you can celebrate your growth together and brainstorm if you get stuck. Starting with one long-term and one short-term goal in each area guards against overwhelm while addressing each of the components of being an intentional caregiver.

Your intentional caregiving goals:

Self-Care

(This is a big area, so I've broken it down into five areas.)

1. Your physical health

    Long-term goal:

    Short-term goals:

    Examples:
    Long-term: I will sleep at least eight hours each night.
    Short-term: I will go to bed by 10 pm four out of seven nights this week.

2. Your mental health

   Long-term goal:

   Short-term goals:

   Examples:
   Long-term: I will make at least one new friend in the next year.
   Short-term: I will go to a support group meeting this week.

3. Your spiritual health

   Long-term goal:

   Short-term goals:

   Examples:
   Long-term: I will find a spiritual community that meets my needs within the next six months.
   Short-term: I will attend an online meditation class on Thursday.

4. Your emotional health

   Long-term goal:

   Short-term goals:

   Examples:
   Long-term: I will learn to manage my stress this year.
   Short-term: I will write down something for which I can be grateful each night before bed for the next month.

5. Your fun/hobbies

   Long-term goal:

   Short-term goals:

   Examples:
   Long-term: I will plant a garden next spring.
   Short-term: I will select and measure a garden spot this week.

Caregiving Tasks

What do you want to improve about the way you provide care for your loved one? You could make a long list, but I suggest no more than three long- and short-term goals at any one time to prevent overwhelm. You can always create more goals in the future.

1. Long-term goal:

    Short-term goals:

2. Long-term goal:

    Short-term goals:

3. Long-term goals:

    Short-term goals:

    Examples:

    Long-term: I will always learn to operate medical equipment with safety and confidence.

    Short-term: I will ask for instruction on how to use the nebulizer today when the nurse visits.

    Long-term: I will help my loved one develop a hobby within the next three months.

    Short-term: I will ask my loved one if they'd like to watch a video on ceramics with me tonight.

Aspirations

An aspiration is something you would like to be, do, or have, but it is harder to measure than a goal. It is something you aim towards or hope for, like aspiring to maintain a positive attitude. I think of aspirations as how I want to be, such as compassionate, understanding, or considerate. They create a positive picture of the future and delightful expectations. They can be idealistic, far-fetched, or even outrageous – very different from SMART goals.

Caregivers should have aspirations for themselves and their loved ones. For example, you might aspire to work in partnership with your loved one, communicate kindly, or laugh with them at least once each day. Consider your aspirations as your dreams put onto paper.

Your personal aspirations:

Examples: To be kinder.
   To feel confident when I am giving injections.
   To be more assertive when I talk with physicians.

Your aspirations for your relationship with your loved one:

Examples: To protect Dad's dignity.

To encourage my wife to make her own choices.

To create some beautiful memories with Mom.

QUESTIONS FOR JOURNALING

Now that you've set some goals and aspirations, how do you feel?

If any of them feel impossible, how can you tweak them to be attainable?

How will you pace yourself to make small, incremental progress on your long-term goals?

The Intentional Caregiver

How can you create some fun around sharing these ideas with your loved one?

Who can support you in achieving your goals and aspirations?

CHAPTER 9
Becoming a Leader

When Karen was in the hospital for all those months after her surgery, a research fellow told her that her cancer had returned. It was a terrible moment for all of us. She did not want to have another round of surgery and chemo. We all worried that she was going to die. It was devastating, especially since she'd experienced so much pain and trauma already. It was the worst day.

We later learned that the research fellow had made a mistake when reading her scans. There was no new cancer. While we were thrilled with the improved diagnosis, Karen lost trust in that physician and asked for him to be removed from her treatment team. She could have pretended everything was fine and choked back her fear every time he entered the room. Instead, she spoke up and asked for what she needed to feel safe. I was incredibly proud of her.

You might wonder why I started a chapter on leadership with a story of how my loved one took charge of her care. Caregiving has many subtle components, and one of the most important is how you can empower your loved one to make their own choices and ask for what they need. When you are a caregiver, you'll be asked to lead in many ways. At times you might need to speak for your loved one and make decisions on their behalf. On other days you will lead by stepping back and supporting your loved one in making difficult choices about their future treatment. Both experiences call for caregiving leadership.

Self-Leadership

When I began my caregiving journey years ago, I was surprised to realize that I was always on duty. When I first started caring for my mother, I did not have time to think things through. She had her stroke, and suddenly my brother and I were her caregivers. It was overwhelming and confusing, as we were young and unprepared. After a few months, I realized that I was always on alert. I slept lightly and never relaxed, even when I had a break. Today Karen uses a monitor at night to ensure she is getting enough oxygen. If the monitor alarm goes off, I need to check to make sure everything is okay. I'm accustomed to it by now, but I'm always listening for the monitor.

Many caregivers I speak with are overwhelmed and broken. They tell me that their lives are a mess – that they cannot sleep or eat well because they give all their attention to their loved one. They worry that they will not be able to continue to provide proper care, and feel guilty about worrying about their health. I understand entirely, and I want to offer a new perspective.

When you are a caregiver, your health and safety become vitally important. I drive more carefully, get checkups, and pay attention to my well-being because if something happens to me, it could harm Karen. I did not realize the value of my health when I cared for my mother, and got very depressed and depleted. Today I am mindful of my health and do the best I can to stay healthy for both of us. It's a form of leadership.

My life changed when I participated in a support group for caregivers and learned that it was a wise idea to take care of myself so that I could take care of Karen. Before that time, I ignored my own needs, even pretending that they did not exist because I felt so guilty that Karen was suffering. I also learned about managing my energy wisely. I used to be the guy who helped. I was the one who took people to the airport, ran errands, and did a lot for my friends and family. I enjoyed it, and yet it was hard for me to say no. Once I became a full-time caregiver, I had to be smarter about my time and energy.

Caregivers have a limited amount of energy available to invest in others. I chose to devote that time and energy to Karen. I've had to learn to say no to requests from others, and I scaled back my participation in community activities. You may face the same choices. Many caregivers try to do it all – maintain their employment, stay active with friends and organizations, and provide care at the same time. That mindset can quickly lead to burnout and caregiver fatigue.

One way to enhance your caregiving abilities is to take a close look at the expectations you are placing on yourself. Make a list of all your obligations and commitments. Then screen them using these questions:

- Are they reasonable?
- Can you maintain all of them and provide care for your loved one?

- Which activities bring you pleasure and satisfaction?
- Are you doing anything out of guilt or obligation?
- What can you stop or delay to free up more energy for your self-care?

It can be challenging to say no to volunteer and social activities. However, when you say no to them, you are saying yes to your loved one and yourself. By making your needs a priority, you are taking a leadership role and setting wise priorities.

Advocating for Your Loved One and You

There will be times when you need to stand up for your loved one. There might be medical professionals who are disrespectful or ignore your loved one's capacity to make choices. You might see signs and symptoms of a medical issue long before others. Insurance companies and home health agencies might deny covered services. In these moments, you will find yourself in a leadership role and advocating for the needs of your loved one. It is almost easy. You love your family member so profoundly that you can find the courage to face any challenge that impacts your loved one. Most caregivers don't think twice about advocating for their loved one.

The more significant challenge is in advocating for you. When others dismiss you as "the spouse," "the parent," or "the caregiver," it can feel more comfortable to say nothing. I encourage you to do your very best to advocate for both your dignity and the dignity of your loved one. When you do, you will increase your self-respect and confidence.

The most effective way to advocate for your loved one and you is to focus on choices. You always have options, as does your loved one. When either of you feels pressured to make quick decisions or do things that you do not want to do, stop. Ask for time to consider options and gain more information. Ask for a second opinion. List your choices and, if possible, discuss them with your loved one. Focusing on making choices removes you and your loved one from the victim role. Lead yourself and your loved one through the process of making decisions, and you'll both feel empowered.

Caregiving Is a Dance

Caregivers become adept at improvising. Each day presents unique challenges. You never know when your loved one will hit a medical or emotional speedbump or when you might come down with the flu. Over time you learn to dance between meeting your loved one's needs and your own. Some days you have to ignore your self-care or planned respite and devote all your attention to your loved one. Other days they may be doing very well and you can give yourself an unexpected break.

Dancing in the moment and being able to adapt to whatever is happening require a flexible mindset. That's another form of leadership. As you grow in experience and confidence in your caregiving role, you'll start to notice that you are developing the skill of responding to whatever arises. A caregiver can create plans and sometimes need to throw them out the window to react to something unexpected.

This ability to dance in the moment requires staying focused in the present moment. If you focus on feelings of guilt over what you did or did not do in the past, or worry about what might happen in the future, it's difficult to notice the blessings and challenges in the present moment. Staying focused in the present moment is a mental discipline that requires strong self-leadership skills. Many try to achieve this focus through meditation or spiritual pursuits. I gained it by caregiving.

I'll be honest; it is very hard to not listen to the part of my mind that tells me I should have done things better in the past or should be anxious about what will happen in the future. I am older than Karen and believe she will outlive me. We are hoping that medical scientists will be able to create an artificial diaphragm so she can breathe independently, but we cannot control the future. When I'm tired, I can easily slip into thinking about the past or the future. Those thoughts do not serve me well.

I've learned to shift out of guilt and worry, when I catch myself with those thought patterns, by celebrating the good things that are happening in the moment. I'll do something fun with Karen, take a walk, read, or even share my feelings with her. Over time we've learned to discuss everything, even when we are having a bad day.

I hope that you realize that you are human. You will have good days and bad days as a caregiver, and that is normal. Being an intentional caregiver means that you notice when you are struggling, and take action to make things better. That's leadership and a skill you will strengthen over time.

QUESTIONS FOR JOURNALING

What are your best leadership qualities?

Which activities or commitments do you need to say no to so you can say yes to your loved one?

How can you support your loved one in making choices?

Are there any new choices you need to make for your well-being?

In what new ways can you dance in the moment and stay focused on today?

CHAPTER 10
Caregiver 911

In this chapter, you'll learn about signs that you need some help. It can be hard to monitor yourself when caregiving. You don't have supervisors or coworkers who can see when you need support, information, or a break. Many caregivers focus all their attention on their loved ones and fail to notice when their own stress is building up. Part of being an intentional caregiver is to pay attention to you while you are providing care to your loved one.

These emotions can alert you to the need for some respite or to make changes in your routines:

- Apathy: when you find yourself feeling bored, blah, and uninterested
- Feeling overwhelmed by the duties and demands of caregiving
- Anger at your loved one, others, or even at the situation
- Guilt
- Extreme anxiety and worry

- Resentment
- Fatigue – either physical or mental exhaustion

It's normal for caregivers to experience these emotions periodically. However, if they linger for more than a day or two and start to interfere with your happiness, it's time to pay attention and take action.

Talking about your feelings and sharing your experiences in a safe, nonjudgmental environment is an effective way to fill your bucket. I found great support in a caregiver's support group offered by our hospital. I also talk with a therapist every month. It is so helpful to be able to offload my emotions and discuss them with those who understand and encourage me. If you cannot leave home, consider joining online groups for caregivers or working virtually with a therapist or coach.

If appropriate, you can also speak with your loved one about how you feel. Giving your loved one the opportunity to nurture you is respectful. If your loved one is stable and the two of you can talk easily like Karen and I do, sharing that you are struggling with some intense emotions can be helpful, especially if it encourages your loved one to share their feelings as well. You can approach this conversation by saying something like:

- I'm feeling cooped up today. What about you?
- I'm worried about your appointment next week. How do you feel?
- I'm so frustrated with the insurance company! Here's what I've tried. Do you have any suggestions?

If your loved one is very ill, or you don't feel it's appropriate to burden them with your feelings, trust your intuition. Your loved one will notice when you are struggling. If they inquire, don't pretend everything is fine. You can decide how much you want to share based on your relationship with your loved one and their status. There is no one-size-fits-all rule.

Siblings and friends can be very supportive. Do your very best to maintain relationships with others. You may only be able to talk by phone or text during times of medical intensity, but those conversations can be very healing for you. Consider keeping regular appointments to see family and friends. You can invite others to a potluck or cook together at home if you are not able to leave the house. If you are able to get away for a bit, meet for coffee or a meal.

For many, journaling is a beneficial way to process painful emotions. Writing about your feelings helps release the pressure from them and find logical solutions to challenges. There is a reason why people have used journaling for centuries. It works!

To give you a taste of the power of journaling about painful emotions, I've created some writing prompts that will help you access feelings that lurk under the surface of your awareness and cause stress. Let yourself complete them fully and honestly. No one will see your answers, grade them, or criticize you. Pour your feelings out onto the page and see if you gain a sense of peace and release when you finish.

- My life feels out of control because...

- I am angry about...

- I'm afraid to tell my loved one…

- I get so bored when…

- I worry when I have to…

- The hardest part of caregiving for me is…

- I resent _____ because…

- I envy _____ because…

- I feel guilty about…

- I really hate…

How do you feel after responding to these prompts? Do you feel less burdened by dark emotions? Do you have any new ideas or insights about how to make your situation more pleasant?

CHAPTER 11

Designing and Nurturing an Alliance with Your Loved One

When my mother came home after her stroke, I was supposed to give her a bed bath. I had no idea how to do that and was embarrassed to see my mother nude. I asked her home health nurse how to go about the process, and she said, "Wash her like an animal." I was mortified and could only imagine how my mother felt to hear such a thing.

During caregiving, you will likely have to help your loved one with toileting, bathing, dressing, and other personal care. You may have to change a colostomy bag, give injections, or clean a feeding tube. These tasks are unfamiliar, a little scary, and potentially embarrassing for you and your loved one.

There may be occasions when you see your loved one dismissed or ignored by medical personnel. They may be treated as if they are not in the room or cannot make their own decisions. Being ill can strip away your dignity, freedom, and self-determination. It's painful for your loved one and for you.

If I had to pick one thing that has made it possible for Karen and me to cope successfully with our situation, it would be the way we work together as a team. We have an alliance and pay attention to make sure that we both have what we need and feel supported. It's taken time to get this right. When Karen came home from the hospital after her surgery, I told her, "Don't worry about going back to work." I meant that she didn't need to worry about money, just to focus on getting well. In hindsight, this was demeaning. I was taking away her choices and making assumptions. Today I would handle it differently. I'd ask, "Can you imagine going back to work in the future? Would you like to?"

Use these ideas to help you form an alliance with your loved one:

- **Keep talking.** Karen and I discuss everything. We make it a point to check in with each other regularly to make sure there are no underlying issues that are causing stress or division. We are normal people, and have disagreements, irritations, and grumpy days. Even when we disagree, we know that we are in this together and will find a way to work things out.

- **Remember the power of choice.** As a busy caregiver, you want the best for your loved one. It can be easy to slip into the habit of making all the decisions. There may be times when your loved one is too ill to make major decisions and you will have to make them, but they will appreciate opportunities to make their own choices as often as possible. It can be little things like whether they would rather watch television or listen to music, and it can be big ones such as a decision to stop treatment or not have a procedure. At the end of the day, if your loved one is an adult, it is their life and they are entitled to live it as they see fit.

- **Use humor.** The first time I had to help Karen with private personal care, we were both uncomfortable. I asked her how she wanted the experience to be. Did she want me to crack jokes, to talk with her, or to stay quiet? She liked the idea of jokes, so I did my best to entertain her. Humor broke the tension for both of us and made the experience enjoyable. Try to inject humor into each day. Watch funny movies or television shows, read a corny joke book, or enjoy funny animal videos. Laughter is healing on many levels.

- **Remind others.** Be mindful of professionals who fail to give your loved one choices or respect. If a professional asks you for a decision, simply say something like, "Dad, what would you like to do?" If there is a healthcare directive, share it with all medical professionals so that they are clear about your loved one's wishes.

- **Be flexible and compassionate.** It's difficult to be sick, especially if you have a long-term, serious medical condition. There will be days when your loved one doesn't want to talk about things, feels angry, or lashes out at you. And there will be days when you experience the same emotions. Those feelings happen in all relationships, but can be intensified by the stress of the situation. Try to put yourself in their shoes, be compassionate with them and with yourself, and trust that things may look brighter tomorrow. When all else fails, hold hands.

- **Avoid assumptions.** It's easy to assume that you know what your loved one wants, thinks, or feels, but assumptions can lead to hurt feelings, mistakes, and rifts. Take the time to ask instead of assuming. Share your thoughts and feelings as well. Your loved one may worry that you want to escape from their illness or that you feel burdened by caregiving. Discussions are always clarifying for both parties.

- **Don't fear feelings.** Some of us were taught that it is bad to be angry, sad, or despairing. Such teachings are common, but ignoring, hiding, or fearing your feelings just turns them into roadblocks. We've all had experiences when we thought we were doing others a favor by putting on a happy face and pretending everything was fine, only to find that it didn't help anyone to suppress our feelings. Caregiving is a very intimate experience. You and your loved one will learn to know each other so deeply that it won't be possible or helpful to hide your feelings. It's healthier to bring them out in the open and share them. Questions are helpful here. Try ones like:
    - You seem a little down. What are you thinking?
    - I'm having a rough day. I hope I won't take it out on you. Can you let me know if I do?
    - What did you like about X? Was there anything you did not care for?
    - I'm worried that I'll hurt you when I lift you. Will you tell me if I need to stop or do things differently?

Anticipate stings. I know that when I need time for myself, it stings Karen a bit. It can feel like desertion when you have to leave your loved one for rest or self-care. Sometimes she says something that stings me as well. Because we have a strong partnership, small stings don't grow into big resentments. We both intentionally work to keep our lines of communication open.

Tips for loved ones who cannot speak: If your loved one cannot speak, see if there is another way they can communicate with you. They might be able to write notes, nod their head, blink their eyes, or squeeze your hand. Experiment and see which communication channels work. My mother could not speak, but we communicated. I would talk to her all the time, tell her what I was doing and why, and ask her questions about her wishes. She was able to nod at times and share her wishes. Even when she could not do that, it was important to keep talking to her and giving her choices. A speech therapist can offer suggestions about assisted communication devices and methods that foster communication in people who are unable to speak.

Develop your alliance over time. Building an alliance with your loved one doesn't happen overnight. Your relationship might be dramatically changed by their medical condition. Give yourself time to learn how to communicate effectively. As time goes by, you may see that your relationship is becoming stronger and more honest. You'll be spending so much time together that you'll both know each other more deeply than before.

I consider myself a very fortunate person. I love Karen dearly and enjoy spending the majority of my time with her. We have fun, share deeply, and can talk about anything, even the hard things. It took time for us to learn to build our alliance, but it was worth it.

If you are struggling to find effective ways to partner with your loved one, consider seeing a therapist. Therapy was beneficial for me. It gave me opportunities to vent and to learn better communication skills. Your loved one also might want to talk with a therapist, member of the clergy, or friend. Loved ones need to vent about caregivers as well!

QUESTIONS FOR JOURNALING

How would you describe your alliance with your loved one?

What steps are you inspired to take after reading this chapter?

Do you recall a time when you empowered your loved one to make choices? How you can foster more such empowerment?

What can you do to bring more laughter into your life?

What is the best part of your relationship with your loved one?

CHAPTER 12
Communication Tips

As a caregiver, you'll be busy providing physical care and attending to the details of life, but one of your most important tasks is to communicate effectively with a wide variety of people. It's very important to communicate clearly to others and pay attention to what is communicated to you and your loved one as well.

Alliances Everywhere

You read about the importance of allying with your loved one in the previous chapter. If you communicate with the goal of allying with everyone you encounter, you and your loved one will have the best possible outcomes. You might not like a particular medical professional or home health aide, but you can find ways to work with them by communicating effectively.

Creating alliances includes respectfully advocating for yourself and your loved one. After Karen's lifesaving surgery and rehabilitation, she looked great. Her medical team was thrilled that the experimental surgery worked so well, and we were so grateful to them; however, I could tell that there was still something wrong. Karen got very tired and was losing weight, but this situation did not seem to concern her medical team. I think they were so delighted that she was alive that her fatigue did not worry them too much.

I started taking her to her doctor's office every week, trying to get some attention for her current situation. It might have seemed like I was a pest, but we just kept making appointments and asking for help with her condition. Finally a physician's assistant suggested we go across the hall and see a pulmonologist. The pulmonologist did some tests and discovered that Karen was retaining CO_2 and needed a ventilator at night. It worked wonders and solved the problem. Through all this, I did my best to communicate respectfully and focus on finding a solution. My job was to be her advocate and not give up until we found it.

As the caregiver, you are an expert in changes in your loved one's condition, especially if those changes are subtle and not apparent during a quick office visit. How you communicate about those changes makes a big difference. Be a respectful, firm, and assertive advocate for your loved one. If you are blustery and demanding, others won't listen to you as attentively as they will if you are humble yet firm, asking for help instead of blaming or letting your anger get the best of you.

Requesting Respect

The medical establishment is intimidating. Everyone has white coats and more degrees than a thermometer. We've been raised to regard physicians as experts who always know the right answer. When my mother was sick, I never questioned anything; I just did what I was told. I've learned that physicians are human like the rest of us and can make mistakes or overlook things in their haste and fatigue. Today I work to build an alliance with every physician, nurse, and medical professional. At heart, all these professionals want the best outcome for your loved one, so you can build on that common goal and help them work with you and your loved one to achieve it.

One of the most empowering ways to request respect for yourself and your loved one is to pay attention to how you are addressed. Medical professionals often don't call you by name. Sometimes we'd hear "Oh, the Grants are here." That bothered me as it sounded like we were things, not people, in their eyes. Medical staff might call you "the husband" (or "the wife"), "the mom" (or "the dad"), "the caregiver," or not address you at all. Your loved one might be asked, "How are we doing today?"

Today I can confidently say, "I'm Geoff, and this is my wife, Karen. Please call us by our first names." When I ask for that level of respect, we get it. It's almost as if the busy medical professional needs a quick reminder that we are people, not just numbers. Names are powerful.

If your loved one cannot speak for themselves, as their advocate you form an alliance with the medical team by alerting them to the best way to communicate with your loved one. If your loved one is verbal, you can assist by asking, for example, "Mom, how would you like your nurse to address you?" When you are a caregiver for your child, let the medical team know your child's preferred name, especially if they use a nickname such as Tommy or Beth instead of the more formal Thomas or Elizabeth. If you are caring for a parent or elder, consider how they would like to be addressed even if they are not able to verbalize that request. Do they prefer being called Mr. Smith or Mrs. Jones or would they rather be called by their first name?

Communicate Your Way

When Karen was in the hospital after her surgery, her parents and siblings were terrific. They came to see her daily. Her family is very athletic and enjoys sporting competitions. When she was struggling, they encouraged her to fight harder and beat her illness. This style of communication was motivating for Karen and a familiar family pattern, but it bothered one of the people on her medical team. We were called in to a family meeting and asked to not be so hard on Karen. This was shocking and upsetting. The team member meant well but was uninformed about who Karen was and what words were motivating for her. We stood together as a family and said that Karen loved this kind of encouragement and had grown up with it all her life from her family and coaches. It helped her, and we were not going to stop.

Always remember that you know your loved one better than any medical professional. Some may need more information to understand the unique person in front of them. No people are alike, and busy staff members can forget this fact at times.

The University of California in San Francisco published these tips for communication with physicians:

- **Be organized.** Write down your questions before your appointment so you can make the most of the appointment time.

- **Keep good records.** Keep a written list of medications, allergies, and medical history for your loved one that you can easily share with physicians.
- **Set the tone.** Tell physicians how much detail you and your loved want as well as about any cultural or religious beliefs that might impact treatment.
- **Be assertive.** Ask questions and request an extended appointment if you need more time to understand the situation.
- **Be understanding.** Remember that your medical team has many patients and demands on their time. Express gratitude and appreciation whenever possible.
- **Ask how they want to be contacted.** Each physician has a preferred way to communicate with patients. Ask and do your best to work within the office guidelines.
- **Take notes.** Take notes or tape-record your visit with the physician.

(https://www.ucsfhealth.org/education/communicating_with_your_doctor)

Communication with Family and Friends

As a caregiver, you'll have many conversations with family and friends. Some of them may be emotionally charged, such as when a decision needs to be made about life support or entering hospice. Some family members might not cope well in stressful situations or medical crises. There might be disagreements between siblings about finances or the best location for a parent's care.

I've found that it is essential to keep the lines of communication open so that everyone is aware of both the positive moments and the areas of concern, and won't feel left out or taken by surprise.

What If You Are Shy?

Some people don't respond well to confrontation, are quiet and reserved by nature, or don't feel comfortable asking for respect or help from strangers. If you are shy, it can make caregiving more challenging, especially when dealing with medical staff, caseworkers, and insurance companies.

A support group can be beneficial in learning how to advocate for yourself and your loved one. I participated in a support group for many years and learned how to communicate in a way that builds alliances and gets what we need from busy professionals. Assertive communication is a skill that you can learn even if you are shy.

However, if you feel too anxious or overwhelmed, ask for help with communicating with others. I know of three brothers who were caring for their father during his cancer. One brother lived in another state and could not provide physical care, so he decided to become the family spokesperson for medical and insurance issues. He attended physician appointments via speaker phone and managed all communications so his younger brothers could focus on the day-to-day tasks. This system worked well for them. You can find a system that works for you. If communication is not your strength, ask for support. You don't have to manage everything perfectly. An intentional caregiver knows to work from strengths and get support wherever needed.

QUESTIONS FOR JOURNALING

How would you like to be addressed by the medical team?

Have you asked your loved one about their communication preferences and how they would like to be addressed? If not, how can you start the conversation?

Can you recall a time when you used assertive communication and had a positive outcome? How can you remember that good experience when it comes time to be assertive with your loved one's medical team?

If you feel intimidated when communicating with medical professionals, how will you become braver or get support from someone else when you need to communicate something difficult?

Which medical professional makes you feel most comfortable and respected? What do they do to make you feel that way, and how can you encourage other professionals to use that communication style?

CHAPTER 13

Empowering Your Loved One

This chapter is one of the most important in *The Intentional Caregiver* because the philosophy in it underpins all the rest of the information. I discovered the importance of empowerment slowly over time as a caregiver. When I focused on empowerment, everything changed – not the outward circumstances, but everything about how I approached caregiving.

One day Karen and I were at a medical appointment. The professional we were working with informed us of several options, then turned to me for a decision. It would have been easy to answer and move on to the next topic for the appointment. Instead I turned to Karen and asked, "What do you think?"

Our loved ones endure many indignities when ill. One of the most subtle is the eroding of their power to choose. They are sometimes treated like children by well-meaning people, including their own caregivers. Of all the things I've learned about in my caregiving journey, the most valuable is the power of choice. To be an intentional caregiver, always look for opportunities to present options.

The power to choose is something we all take for granted until it is stripped away from us. To empower your loved one, respect their ability to decide. You might need to remind others that your loved one is in charge of their life and can make their own choices. I can't pretend to understand how Karen feels about her medical condition. But I can resist the temptation to treat her like a child.

In everyday life, empowering the power to choose might sound like this:

- Would you like to go to therapy on Mondays or Wednesdays?
- What would you like to have for dinner?
- Shall we go for a drive this morning or would tomorrow be better?
- What do you think about your lab results?
- Are you in the mood for a movie or would you rather listen to music?

It's About Control

When someone becomes seriously ill, they lose control over their environment. Their body is not cooperating and may not be able to do the things it used to do. In some cases, their mind is impaired, either by medications or by their condition. Medical facilities further stifle self-determination. Patients are told what to wear, when to eat, what they can do, and even when they can sleep.

As an intentional caregiver, one of your most important roles is to find ways to give some control back to your loved one by offering choices. Remind them that they always have a choice. That is empowering and respectful. Consider things like:

- Would you like an extra blanket?
- Is there anyone you would like me to call?
- Shall I shut the door or leave it open?
- May I hold your hand?
- Do you want to take a walk or rest a while?

If your loved one is nonverbal or in a medical crisis, their ability to choose may be impaired for a time. Even when you doubt that they can hear you or communicate, offer choices anyway. Sometimes they can experience a window of clarity when they can communicate a choice to you by nodding their head or squeezing your hand. Even if they cannot respond, the act of offering options reminds everyone that your loved one has power in their life.

Anticipate a Better Future Together

Karen is not able to drive at this time because of her medical condition. That did not stop us from enjoying a car show. I asked her about what kind of car she'd like to drive when she is able to resume driving. It was fun to think about the future together and a way to show her that I believed she would continue to gain strength.

We enjoy talking together and often spend time planning things we'd like to try. I'm aware that some things are frightening for her, such as traveling out of town. That does not stop us from considering taking a trip together. Karen can decide where she'd like to go and other details of the trip, even if it is just a hope for the future. It's empowering for both of us to think about the potential.

Gradually Promote Independence

Recently I realized that I was becoming annoying by continually asking Karen how she was feeling. I was unknowingly treating her like she was fragile when she is one of the strongest people I know. We made an agreement that she could ask for help at any time, and I'd be there, but I would try to curb my habit of constantly asking if she needed anything.

Everyone wants to feel respected and as if they are contributing. It is a wise idea to ask your loved one to help with tasks around the house as they are able. Start with things like:

- Folding laundry
- Planning meals
- Chopping vegetables
- Ordering medications or supplies online
- Sorting the junk drawer or mail

Find things your loved one can do and then adapt the tasks around their physical or cognitive limitations. For example, Karen fills the top of the dishwasher but cannot bend, so I do the bottom half. We grocery shop together, but she is in charge of creating the list.

Start with one thing that can promote their independence. Once that is mastered, add something else. If your loved one has access to an occupational therapist, the therapist can help adapt activities of daily living around any limitations.

Promoting independence might be challenging for you. There will be times when your loved one will struggle, and it might seem easier and kinder to just put their socks on for them. However, doing so will subtract from their independence. Instead, let them try to do as much as they can, knowing that their abilities will change based on their medical status. It's a delicate balance between helping and hovering. You won't get it right every time, but you'll learn to work in partnership with your loved one.

Acknowledge Trying

When you've been very ill, it can be exhausting to shower or even brush your teeth. You cannot control how much your loved one can do for themselves; you can applaud their efforts. A simple "Wow, you stood for longer today than ever before" shows your loved one that you realize how hard they are trying.

Your loved one might lose abilities as their illness progresses. Even when they can no longer do things for themselves, you can praise their efforts. Something as simple as turning over in bed or raising an arm to assist with dressing can be a monumental effort. When you notice and acknowledge those efforts, you are respecting your loved one and empowering them.

The mindset of empowerment can make the experience of caregiving more rewarding for you and for your loved one. Providing choices, respect, self-determination, independence, and acknowledgment costs nothing and produces excellent rewards. Keep this as a general principle and remember that you are trying new things, too. You'll make mistakes often, perhaps expecting too much or too little from your loved one. Acknowledge that you are doing your best, apologize, forgive yourself, and try again. It's all part of the journey.

QUESTIONS FOR JOURNALING

What choices can you give your loved one?

Do you find it easy to see opportunities to contribute? If not, who can help you?

What potential future can you discuss with your loved one today?

How are you inspired to foster independence in your loved one?

What efforts can you praise?

CHAPTER 14
Asking For and Receiving Help

After Karen's surgery, she had grueling chemotherapy sessions. The side effects were terribly painful, and she reached a point at which she wanted to stop treatment. I tried to talk with her and provide encouragement, but could not find the right words. Then her father spoke with her and told her something that gave her the power to continue. We have been very blessed because Karen's family is incredibly supportive and will do anything to help us.

When I was my mother's caregiver, my brother and I had little support from others, partly because we had few nearby family resources and partly because we were young and did not know how to effectively ask for caregiving support. Our gender also influenced us. Many girls grew up changing diapers and caring for children, especially when we were growing up in the 1970s and '80s. Boys were taught to be strong, independent, and mow the lawn or do other outdoor chores. And yet, according to a study by AARP, in late 2014 men provided 40 percent of family caregiving. (https://www.aarp.org/content/dam/aarp/ppi/2015/caregiving-in-the-united-states-2015-report-revised.pdf)

Whether you are a male or female caregiver, you need help. It is impossible to shoulder all the responsibility for providing full-time care for your loved one, especially when their medical condition lasts more than a few weeks. Well-meaning people will say, "Call me if I can help," but it's challenging to take them up on that request. You might even decline help that is offered out of embarrassment or shame that you can't do everything alone.

The first step in getting support is to admit to yourself that you are not superman or superwoman. It is natural to want to be strong for your loved one. You don't want to worry them or distract them from their healing journey. You also may fear that someone else will not have the information or skill needed to provide care safely. You might want to avoid burdening others or think that it is just easier to suck it up and do things on your own. Your mental resistance to asking for and receiving help is often the biggest obstacle you face.

Consider the cost of that thinking. You run the risk of compromising your health to the point that you end up in the hospital with no one ready to step in and care for your loved one. You deprive your loved one of seeing other faces, and you stop others from contributing when they truly wish to. You never know who might make a positive difference for your loved one. A friend, neighbor, or even a cousin might say something that gives your loved one new strength and empowerment. It honestly does take a village to provide care. Once you accept that idea, you'll have a much easier time asking for help.

Many of us were not taught how to ask for help. We wait for others to notice that we are overburdened and ask to help. Unfortunately people are not mind-readers and may overlook signs that you are getting exhausted or need support. You will need to ask. Over time asking for help becomes more comfortable.

Barbara and Jim Twardowski wrote in *Forbes* about how she had to learn to ask for help when she became disabled. She offers these wise suggestions:

- **Clarify what you need –** making lists is a great idea.
- **Brainstorm possible solutions with friends and family.**
- **Build a support network.** Include neighbors, community organizations, and contacts from religious organizations. You have big and small needs, so having a list of people to ask helps. You will not overburden anyone if many hands are helping.
- **Match talents to needs.** Perhaps a neighbor can let you know when she is getting groceries and is willing to pick up a few things for you. A family member who loves music might enjoy coming over to listen to music while you take a break. Your cousin who loves to cook might be delighted to bring over a casserole once a week. When people are using their talents, helping is easy and enjoyable for them.
- **Make specific requests.** It is much easier to ask someone to help with laundry once a week or to help you build a ramp on Saturday than just asking for general help.
- **Stay organized.** It's up to you, or someone you delegate, to keep track of who is doing what tasks. Perhaps a family member would enjoy this task. There are several ways

to organize volunteers. You can use a simple notebook or an online solution such as TakeThemAMeal.com or LotsaHelpingHands.com.

- **Say thanks.** People will want to help if they feel appreciated. You can send a quick thank you email or text, send a card, or make a phone call. If your loved one is able, they might want to take on the task of thanking others.

(https://www.forbes.com/sites/nextavenue/2016/09/02/8-tips-to-ask-for-the-caregiving-help-you-need/#51347f4b16d6)

If you and your loved one are part of a religious or spiritual organization, you can ask others to pray for you. Members of your spiritual family can be good visitors and helpers if you ask.

If there are people in your life who are not able to help physically because they live far way, have health challenges of their own, or have little time, they might be willing to contribute money, order groceries online, or send greeting cards to your loved one.

Consider Your Needs, Too

You might need someone to help you if your loved one falls or to go to dinner with you when you have the opportunity to go out. It's helpful to have people ready to support you as well as your loved one. Do you have a friend who will let you vent? Is there someone who will encourage you or make you laugh? Who will sit with you when your loved one is in surgery or intensive care?

When you are building your support team, ensure that you have support for yourself along with support in meeting the needs of your loved one. The more support you have, the easier it is to care for your loved one and the happier you both will be.

Outside Options

Your loved one may qualify for assistance at home. Explore options for home health aides funded by insurance coverage, Medicare/Medicaid, and state and local programs. Ask social workers and case managers for resources. Reach out to the local Agency on Aging, disease-specific groups such as the Cancer Society, and hospice care centers if your loved one has a terminal illness.

If you have the financial resources, you can hire a home health aide or people to assist with cooking, cleaning, or yard work. Do an internet search for home health agencies in your community. Your local library or public health department might have lists of groups and agencies that can assist. My mother went to a day program for seniors that provided stimulation and much-needed respite for my brother and me.

Keep Communication Open

As you ask for and receive help from others, do your best to maintain communication with them. When your loved one has a significant setback or even an improvement, let people know so they can send good thoughts or celebrate with you. You are allying with these people, and they will appreciate appropriate updates and information as things change. If this seems too taxing, enlist a helper to handle this communication for you.

Once you start thinking about specific tasks that others can do to lighten your load, you'll find many more ideas coming to mind.

QUESTIONS FOR JOURNALING

How do you feel about asking for help?

Who is helping you now, and how might you channel their help more effectively?

What tasks would be the easiest to delegate to others?

Does your loved one miss contact with friends or family members? If so, can you facilitate a visit or phone call?

Can you think of one new person who can provide help? How can you find the willingness to ask them for help this week?

CHAPTER 15
Forgiving Yourself and Others

Caregivers cope with guilt almost every day. You can feel guilty for lots of reasons, including the guilt caused by:

- Being healthy while your loved one suffers
- Feeling envious of others' more carefree lives
- Frustration, boredom, or anger
- Missing an appointment or forgetting to take paperwork along
- Wondering what life would have been like if your loved one was not ill
- Resentment that others are not helping you
- Conflict with your loved one or other family members
- Mistakes with equipment or medications
- Overlooking a symptom or change in status or not communicating it to your loved one's medical team
- Falls from the bed or the wheelchair
- Causing pain while transferring or dressing

I participate in some online forums for caregivers and notice that many are suffering under a heavy load of guilt. It is part of the caregiving journey; however, you don't have to allow guilt to cause you pain or stress.

Researchers studying caregiving have even developed a Caregiver Guilt Questionnaire that looks at five types of caregiver guilt:

1. Guilt about making mistakes or doing wrong
2. Guilt about failing to meet the challenges of caregiving
3. Guilt about negative feelings about caregiving
4. Guilt about self-care
5. Guilt about neglecting other family members

https://www.cambridge.org/core/journals/international-psychogeriatrics/article/validation-of-the-caregiver-guilt-questionnaire-cgq-in-a-sample-of-british-dementia-caregivers/E1D2CDE2A18115436D05BAFF39B9E383

Proper Responsibility

It is helpful to make a distinction between what you are responsible for and what you are not. You are responsible for providing care in the best way you can. You are not a trained medical professional, so you are not responsible for knowing how to do things correctly the first time. It took a lot of practice before I felt comfortable with some of Karen's medical equipment.

You are always concerned about your loved one's health, but you cannot control it. It would be so lovely if you could snap your fingers and your loved one would be restored to glowing good health. Unfortunately, even with excellent caregiving, your loved one may suffer setbacks, need to enter a care center, or even pass away. You are not responsible for that, even though you might feel guilty.

It can be easy to have a fantasy in your mind of being the ideal caregiver – always patient, kind, giving, and wise. That fantasy doesn't work well in the real world of caregiving. Being a perfect caregiver is impossible. There will be days when you are exhausted or do not feel well. On those days you might make errors, snap at your loved one, or be grumpy. You are human. It is normal to have off days. Remember the days before your loved one's illness? You had times of conflict and disagreement then. Conflict is just part of everyday life.

Forgive Yourself

When you're feeling guilty, it can be beneficial to write about your feelings or discuss them with a therapist, coach, or trusted friend. Aim to answer these questions so you can understand your emotions:

- Why do I feel guilty today?
- Did I do something that requires an apology?
- Did I make an error because I need more training?
- Am I feeling resentful or upset because I am tired and need a break?
- Can I discuss this with my loved one?
- What would make me feel better now?

Think through the answers to these questions, and then let go of the situation. If you've made a mistake, admit it, make amends, or get help so it doesn't happen again, and then let it go. Ruminating over errors makes it more likely that you will make more of them. Guilt is not a productive emotion. It zaps your energy instead of energizing you. When you feel guilty, it is a signal that you need to make a change. Perhaps you need more help, respite care, or some fun with your loved one.

Forgiving yourself is a powerful and healthy thing to do. Caregiving provides plenty of opportunities to learn to forgive yourself. Consider it a training ground for self-compassion and forgiveness.

Forgive Others

When my mother had her stroke, other relatives were not able to participate in her care. It was hard not to be angry or disappointed when my brother and I were so overwhelmed. There will be times in your caregiving journey when you are bitterly disappointed in others. People you expect to support you might disappear. Siblings might disagree with the decisions you make for your parent's care. In extreme cases, others might accuse you of taking advantage of your loved one, just being around for the inheritance, or deciding to move your loved one to a care facility unnecessarily.

Unfortunately guilt and grief can lead to many problems within families. Others who are not involved in day-to-day caregiving might not understand your need for respite or they might disagree with your decisions about care. We have all heard sad stories of siblings fighting about who would care for aging parents or whether or not to continue life support.

When you feel wronged by others, or worse, when you think they have hurt your loved one, the best thing you can do is forgive them and move on. Forgiveness does not mean you approve of their actions or you will pretend the behavior did not happen. It only means you are releasing the burden of feeling angry and are willing to let the situation go. If you believe in God or karma, you may hope that the offending person experiences a consequence from their choices, but you are not going to put your emotional energy into holding a grudge, getting revenge, or staying angry.

Forgiving can be very difficult. It can take time to let the powerful feelings subside. But it helps you feel better. It's a worthwhile endeavor.

Try these ideas from forgiveness researcher Dr. Robert Enright:

- Believe that forgiveness is possible.
- Choose to forgive.
- Notice how your anger about the situation is harming you.
- Think about the other person and how they may have been hurt.
- Remember that you are both human.
- Soften your heart and aim for compassion.

(https://www.powerofpositivity.com/psychologists-explain-truly-forgive-someone-let-go)

Remember that old song, "Haven't Got Time for the Pain"? As a caregiver, you have limited emotional energy. Is it worth the energy it takes to hold on to your anger? I propose that you "haven't got time for the pain," and my recommendation is to do your best to forgive others even if they don't apologize, admit their mistake, or even have contact with you. You can forgive someone without discussing it with them.

Forgiveness is for you, to lighten your load and free up energy that you can devote to your loved one and self-care.

QUESTIONS FOR JOURNALING

What do you feel guilty about?

If someone else is trying to make you feel guilty about your caregiving, how can you address this?

What might change if you could forgive yourself and experience less guilt?

Who can you discuss your feelings of guilt and anger with?

Who might you need to forgive?

CHAPTER 16

Caregiving While Your Loved One Is at a Medical Facility

When your loved one is in the hospital or another medical facility, your role shifts a bit. Instead of providing all the physical care, your job is now to enhance their quality of life and be their advocate. Being in a large medical complex is intimidating and stressful for both loved ones and caregivers. There are strict rules, people in white who are always in a hurry, and all kinds of strange noises and equipment. Your loved one is facing surgery or a health crisis. It's never a comfortable situation.

Working with the Team

Your loved one will have a team of medical professionals including physicians, therapists, nurses, and social workers. Each of these professionals brings different viewpoints and information to the situation. Many are exhausted and are under hefty demands in their work. It is always wise to treat them with respect and appreciation. The old saying is true: You can often get more with honey than with vinegar. Thank them all and pay extra attention to the nurses. Most nurses are kind people who want to help. They can often answer questions or communicate your concerns to physicians.

At the same time, don't be afraid to speak up when there is a problem or you have a concern. If there is a problem with your loved one's room, meals, or nursing care, ask to speak to the nursing supervisor. It is possible to have a nurse or assistant reassigned to another patient if you feel there is a substantial conflict or you are uncomfortable with them. All medical facilities are organized around a hierarchy with a clear chain of command to address issues. Start with nurses, then the floor supervisor, then the nursing supervisor, and finally consult an administrator if you cannot resolve the problem. Most facilities are required to inform you during the admissions process of patient rights and how to communicate concerns.

Some physicians are purposefully vague and reluctant to give clear answers about a prognosis because they are afraid of lawsuits. It can be difficult for some of them to deliver difficult news or suggest stopping treatment. Do your best to be present when physicians make rounds so you can ask questions as needed. I always ask the nurses when the physicians generally make their rounds. At most hospitals it is in the early morning hours.

If your loved one has multiple physicians, watch to see that all are on the same page and communicating with each other. Some facilities employ hospitalists – physicians who work only in the hospital and do not follow the patient after discharge. If you are concerned that information is not flowing correctly between hospitalists and your regular physicians, discuss it with your loved one's lead physician or primary care physician.

To make the admission process more straightforward, prepare a notebook or file with insurance information, medical history, medications, a copy of your loved one's driver's license or other identification, contact information for primary care physicians, and any advance directives. You will need all this information for every admission, so having all the paperwork organized and easily accessible is very helpful, especially if your loved one needs to be admitted in an emergency situation. Some people put this information in a colored notebook or file. Others place it on an iPad or smartphone. Find a method that works best for you.

Choices and Distraction

When your loved one is a patient, someone else is dictating what they do, what they eat, and even when they can get out of bed. It's very empowering to find ways to give your loved one choices. Ask questions like:

- Would you like to call your friend and chat for a while?
- Can I bring you something from home?
- Shall we watch TV or do you want to listen to music?
- Would you like to take a walk or go for a spin in your wheelchair?
- Can I bring you a magazine from the gift shop?

Every moment that you can distract your loved one is one less moment when they are afraid. When Karen was in the hospital for all those months, I did everything I could to distract her from her situation and improve her quality of life. One of the first things we did was to play checkers. We never played checkers at home, but someone gave her a small checkerboard, and we enjoyed it regularly. Consider these ideas:

- Watching television shows or online videos about favorite hobbies such as cooking, gardening, travel, or history
- Playing cards or board games. Jenga can be a lot of fun played on a bed tray.
- Working word games, puzzle books, word searches, or Sudoku
- Watching favorite movies or films with easy-to-follow plots
- Listening to favorite music
- Looking at photo albums or family photos
- Reading aloud to your loved one
- Holding hands
- Talking about happy memories or plans for the future
- Knitting, coloring, doing small puzzles, or doing easy handicrafts
- Watching funny sitcoms. The short format of a sitcom can be ideal because it requires less concentration than a movie. I recommend classics like *I Love Lucy*.
- Supply anything that connects your loved one to a favorite hobby. I bought Karen a small camera to use in the hospital. You can take in car magazines, travel brochures, or even cookbooks with lots of photos. Use your imagination and creativity.

You can provide comfort by bringing in a favorite robe, blanket, socks, or stocking hat. Hospitals can be very chilly. It's nice to decorate the room with family photos or stuffed animals. Don't forget pictures of your pets. If your loved one receives cards or letters, take them in as well.

If your loved one wants to see a particular friend or someone from your religious organization, call and ask them to visit. There may be times when your loved one does not want any visitors at all. That's another choice you can provide.

Amy Goyer, writing in AARP magazine, suggested some additional comforts for hospital stays including:

- Chargers for electronic devices
- Healthy snacks
- Aromatherapy room sprays
- Lip balm and lotions
- Good quality tissues
- Saline solution or Vicks® VapoRub™ for combating dry hospital air
- Small flashlight
- Sleep mask
- White noise machine or soothing nature sounds to play on an electronic device to cover the hospital sounds

http://blog.aarp.org/2012/04/17/caregiving-hospitals-caring-for-parents

Take Care of You, Too

Sitting in a hospital can be lonely and tiring for loved ones and caregivers. It is crucial that you pay attention to your self-care, too. Remember that you will have a lot to do after discharge, so you cannot afford to become depleted during hospitalizations.

It can be tempting to believe that you must be with your loved one around the clock. That may be true in emergency situations, but when your loved one is out of danger, do your best to give yourself time to sleep, shower, and eat properly. Consider going out for a walk when your loved one is napping or attending therapy sessions. Except in emergencies, it's best that you go home once they are ready to sleep for the night so you can get your rest, too, and return early the next morning for physician rounds.

If the facility is too far from your home to commute, ask if there are any arrangements with nearby hotels for family members. Pack a suitcase for your needs as well as for your loved one. Wear comfortable clothing and bring things that will help you pass the time while you are waiting.

Most facilities have chapels, meditation areas, and green spaces where you can get a bit of peace and relaxation. There will be times when you need to leave your loved one's room, so use those times to explore the grounds or get a meal. Just getting outdoors for a few minutes can be very restorative.

Ask for help. Call on friends and family members to give you respite, sit with you during surgeries and procedures, and bring things you need but didn't have time to get. People want to help. Offering a concrete suggestion for something you need allows them to assist in a meaningful way. You are in a stressful situation. Even having someone come and eat a meal with you strengthens and empowers you. You are giving a lot to your loved one, so let others give to you, too.

QUESTIONS FOR JOURNALING

In what ways are you comfortable or uncomfortable about advocating for your loved one?

How do the ideas about distracting your love one while they are at a medical facility inspire you?

What would your loved one find comforting or entertaining while at a medical facility?

Do you have an admission notebook or file ready? What do you need to do to get that completed?

Who can support you when your loved one is in a medical facility?

CHAPTER 17
Logistics and Planning for Emergencies

When Karen came home after her surgery, she had a feeding tube and several pieces of medical equipment that enabled her to breathe. It was very intense for both of us. I had to learn how to hook up all the equipment, use it correctly, order medications and supplies, and continuously monitor her condition. Her health was very fragile at the time.

Frankly we were both scared. It was a miracle that Karen survived her surgery, but now we had to figure out how to keep her alive and allow her to regain her strength. Without the equipment to breathe for her and give her nutrition, she would not be able to survive. The machines had to run several times each day. While they were running, they were very noisy and intrusive. I had to learn to hook them all up quickly and was concerned I'd make a terrible mistake or forget one of the steps.

She was on many medications and required lots of supplies. I placed orders each month, and when the orders arrived there were boxes and boxes of things to be organized and stored.

I was surprised at how overwhelming it was to deal with the inventory of supplies.

During this time of about six months, all I could do was keep up with the machines, supplies, and medical appointments. There was no time to exercise, go out to lunch, or do things for me. When your loved one is in a very fragile state, you might have to put your own needs aside for a while. I realize that statement seems to contradict everything you have learned thus far in the book, but if you are already a caregiver you know firsthand that there are times when you must devote the vast majority of your time, energy, and life to your loved one. You can still be intentional about how you approach those experiences. Remind yourself that you are choosing to focus on your loved one temporarily until they get stronger. It is a choice that you make from love to forego your time for fun and relaxation.

Tips for Intense Times

During this six-month period, I began to appreciate the incredible responsibility of being Karen's caregiver. It was up to me to keep her alive on a day-to-day basis. I was on duty 24/7 and continuously listening for a problem with a machine or a change in her health status. It can be quite a challenge to maintain your emotional and physical health during intense periods of caregiving such as that. This is when you learn that caregiving is not as easy as preparing meals and doing laundry, although those things must be done, too. These tips will help:

- **Learn everything you can.** All of Karen's medical equipment had an 800 number on it with help available 24/7. A liaison came to our house to teach me the operational procedures. I asked lots of questions and did not hesitate to call for help if I had a problem or something did not seem right.

- **Focus on high-priority responsibilities.** During that time, I had to devote most of my time to the equipment and Karen's care. I was not able to spend time on much else and had to make peace with the idea that some non-essential things would be delayed for a while.
- **Create routines that decrease the number of things you have to remember.** I was tired, stressed, and afraid I'd forget things. It helped to create routines that reminded me of when to do things. Finding a routine and then following it as closely as possible gave the days a rhythm and predictability that was calming for both Karen and me.
- **Stay organized.** When I kept all the supplies organized, I did not need to waste time hunting for things. I also kept lists of things I had to do so that I would not have to rely on my memory. It can seem like it will take too much of your precious time to organize, but doing so will save more time in the long run.
- **Ask for and be receptive to help.** If you have friends or family members who can help by preparing meals or doing housekeeping or laundry, it will free your time to focus on your loved one.
- **Consider training another person on the equipment if appropriate.** In our situation, I was able to devote all my time to taking care of Karen. If that is not possible in your situation, or the intensity lasts for a long time, draft a trusted friend or family member to be trained

in equipment operation so that you have a backup in case of emergencies. The equipment supplier or home health nurse will provide that training if required.

- **Work in partnership with your loved one.** Karen was able to operate some of her equipment as she gained strength. We worked together on the setup so she could tell me if something did not feel right. It was very helpful to have her partnership. We conquered it together, and that felt really good for both of us.

- **Choose "cruise control."** During times of crisis, you might have to put your self-care on the back burner and focus on getting the crucial tasks completed. This is not a failure. Instead it is a choice. Remembering that you are choosing to prioritize your loved one's needs ahead of yours for a time will help you manage stress and work from the power of your intention.

- **Focus on moving forward one day at a time.** During intense times, thinking about the distant future can compound stress for you and your loved one. Instead, concentrate on getting through each day with the hope that the following day will be a little better. There will be times of setbacks and speedbumps. Anticipate them and don't be alarmed when they appear. Look for and celebrate improvements, whether in your loved one's condition or in the skills you are developing to manage the demands.

- **Trust the process.** Learning to operate medical equipment, giving treatments, and administering injections are new skills for most caregivers, but you can learn them. The professionals who instruct you want you to succeed and are trained in how to teach laypeople. Realize that you will gain ability and ease over time. Soon you'll be able to perform caregiving tasks confidently.

- **Listen to your intuition.** When your gut tells you something is wrong, listen and act. You know your loved one better than anyone else. If you have a sense that something is wrong, ask for help. You will become attuned to subtle things that medical professionals can miss.

- **Laugh!** It is vitally important that you and your loved one share connection and laughter during intense times. We found that watching silly movies or television shows was helpful, as well as telling jokes and sharing humorous experiences.

Everyday Preparedness

We live in New England where the power often goes out during winter storms. This is a big challenge as Karen requires electricity for her medical equipment. We've learned to watch the weather and proactively prepare, just in case.

I've found several hotels with generators and accessible rooms nearby. I keep plenty of gasoline in the car and extra medications and supplies. If we need to leave our home during a storm, we have a plan and know that it will work. The time it took to create that plan was minimal compared to the peace of mind it provides.

Consider what challenges you may encounter. Do you live in an area with severe weather or wildfire danger? Where might you go if you need to evacuate your home? Do you have neighbors, friends, or family who can help? Would a generator be useful?

Take the time to talk with your loved one about preparing for disasters and severe weather. Create a plan together. Remember that old saying, "When you prepare for the worst, the best often happens." I hope that you never have to use your emergency plans, but if you do you'll be happy you created those plans in advance.

QUESTIONS FOR JOURNALING

If you have been caregiving for a while, describe a time when you felt overwhelmed taking care of your loved one. How did you learn to overcome those feelings?

What medical equipment or procedures intimidate you?

Who can provide support to help you gain confidence?

What are your plans for emergency situations?

How can you bring more humor into your caregiving so that you can diffuse tension?

CHAPTER 18
Fostering Fun and Creativity

When your loved one is ill, they lose some of their autonomy and control. In the hospital, someone else dictates when they eat or get out of bed. They are told what to do and what they can no longer do. Their health condition can limit their choices and freedom. Most people who have health concerns can no longer leave home spontaneously, go hiking, or take exotic vacations. There are many losses of independence and personal power.

As an intentional caregiver, you have an excellent opportunity to help your loved one enjoy their time. I firmly believe that the more a loved one is happy and distracted from their pain, the better their quality of life is. And it makes life more enjoyable for you, too.

Karen has developed a passion for photography in the last few years. All the lovely photos in this book are hers. She spent time researching cameras and taking photography classes online and at a local photography shop. We spend as much time as possible visiting places where she can take photos of flowers, nature, and other things that catch her eye. Each year she creates a calendar of her photos and gives them to family and friends. She even created a website with her photography. She has developed a real talent, and it fills her with joy. When she's shooting photos, she pushes herself physically and seems stronger because she's focusing on what she loves.

There are many opportunities to help your loved one develop a pleasing quality of life even if they have health limitations. All it takes is a little creativity and thoughtfulness. Enhancing creativity is one of my favorite parts of caregiving. It's my goal to bring as much fun into our lives as possible. Caregivers often get so bogged down in the chores, worries, and demands that they forget that moments of fun and joy make life worth living for loved ones and caregivers.

Simple Pleasures

I know a man who is quite ill and confined to his bed most of the time. His family hung bird feeders near his windows and got him a set of binoculars so he could watch birds. Over time he started to learn about birds online and through books from the local library. When he has visitors, he can talk about the birds he's seen instead of his medical condition.

Our grandparents were experts at finding ways to enjoy life. Think back to some of the things your grandparents liked and you'll have a wealth of ideas to explore with your loved one. Here are some of my favorites:

- Jigsaw puzzles
- Playing cards or board games

- Reading aloud to each other
- Telling stories and jokes
- Music in all forms – singing, listening to recordings, or playing an instrument
- Caring for houseplants or gardening
- Handicrafts such as knitting, woodworking, or painting
- Walking around the backyard or neighborhood
- Visiting with neighbors
- Preparing a meal together or baking cookies
- Crossword puzzles and word search or other games
- Sharing stories about childhood adventures
- Planning future home-improvement projects

Tour Your Hometown

Karen and I love to go out for ice cream. It seems like nothing, but getting out of the house can be a pleasant change of pace. We've also discovered many activities in our area that don't require much money but provide much enjoyment. Before Karen's illness, we were so busy with our lives that we overlooked many opportunities such as:

- **The public library:** Regular visits to the library keep us stocked with books, magazines, and movies.
- **Schools:** We've had fun attending plays and concerts at our high schools and nearby universities. While we can't easily go to Broadway to see a show, we can still enjoy musicals.
- **Animal shelters:** There is an animal shelter near our home that welcomes visitors and volunteers. We enjoy seeing their bunnies.

- **Parks:** When was the last time you sat in a park? We love to visit local and state parks to enjoy nature.
- **Museums:** We enjoy touring historic homes, gardens, and a local natural history museum that has a butterfly house.
- **Pool halls:** It's a lot of fun to play pool and it doesn't require much physical strength or stamina.
- **Religious organizations:** Churches often offer free musical performances, events, and group activities along with religious services.
- **Movie theatres:** An afternoon matinee is fun and affordable.
- **Restaurants:** Order favorite foods for home delivery or go out to eat, trying out new restaurants and venues you haven't yet visited.
- **Hardware stores:** Looking at paint samples, seeds, or bathroom fixtures can be enjoyable.

Explore Technology

The internet brings the world to your loved one even if they must be in bed. Consider an iPad or tablet if your loved one lacks the strength to sit at a desk or manage a bulky laptop. One of the best things about the internet is that it fosters curiosity and discovery. Everyone can find something of interest online. Consider:

- Using Skype or Zoom for video chats with friends and family
- YouTube has videos that teach you almost anything, from cooking to fly fishing.

- Becoming an armchair traveler by selecting a country you'd like to visit and researching it online. You can learn about the history and culture, look at photos, and watch videos from others who have traveled there.
- Researching family history
- Listening to audiobooks
- Downloading ebooks
- Watching movies and then googling the cast to learn more about them
- Participating in online groups related to an interest or your loved one's medical condition
- Using social media to share photos and connect with others

Hobbies

Hobbies can be life-enhancing for both caregivers and their loved ones. Everyone has an interest in something. Whether you watch cooking shows, use a telescope to view the stars, or study ancient history, engaging in a hobby distracts you from pain, boredom, and isolation. As a caregiver, you know what your loved one enjoys. Find ways to bring that hobby into their lives whether they are at home or in a medical facility. My mother loved to spend time with friends, so I took her to a day program to see new faces.

Other caregivers have shared stories with me of visiting county fairs, taking drives, watching programs about history or science, creating scrapbooks, looking at old photos, and sorting out the contents of a tackle box. One person loved to solve mysteries, so he and his caregiver would talk about books and movies to uncover the clues and try to answer "Who dun it?" Others subscribed to new magazines, perused catalogs, or set up a sewing machine for quilting.

Your loved one has a variety of interests that can develop into life-enhancing hobbies. It might require trying several things before discovering the best options. Talk with your loved one about what they would like to try. If it sounds like it might be challenging, problem-solve together to work around limitations, either with their health or finances. Part of the fun of having a hobby is the preparation time it requires.

Chores

This might sound strange, but it can be very fulfilling to complete chores. Loved ones often feel guilty that their caregivers are shouldering so many of the responsibilities at home. Consider breaking down household tasks into smaller steps so both of you can work together to complete them. The following examples don't require excessive physical strength and can be done seated or even in bed:

- Folding laundry
- Matching socks
- Peeling vegetables and fruits
- Paying bills and organizing finances
- Stamping envelopes
- Sorting coupons, mail, magazines, and paperwork
- Planning menus and grocery lists
- Organizing the junk drawer or part of a closet
- Shopping online for groceries, medications, and clothing

- Creating lists for holiday events or upcoming celebrations
- Putting medications into pill caddies

Holidays

Holidays can bring joy or a stark reminder of all the things your loved one can no longer do. It's important to pay attention to holidays and discuss what would be the most enjoyable activities for your loved one; there might be some holidays that they don't want to celebrate, or times when a health speedbump disrupts planned events. Spend time together planning what you'd like to do. You can adapt traditional activities to fit with your loved one's stamina and energy. Consider these ideas:

- Make each other cards instead of going out to purchase gifts.
- Use online shopping services.
- Watch favorite holiday movies.
- Create homemade gifts together for family and friends.
- Invite a few friends or relatives for an easy pot luck or barbecue at your home.
- Drive to view holiday lights or fireworks.
- Invite carolers to sing outside your loved one's window.
- Donate to a charity that helps others.
- Plan a fantasy celebration using online videos and websites, such as a trip around the world.

Remember to Dance in the Moment

Caregiving can be unpredictable. One day your loved one is full of energy and the next may be laid low with an infection. As you work together and create plans for fun, plan loosely so that neither of you feels pressured. Be willing to change plans quickly as needed. You might look forward to an outing to the movies but then not be able to go. Find a substitute such as a movie marathon with popcorn at home. If you are on a hike and your loved one becomes fatigued, it's okay to go home early. If your loved one is feeling great on a pretty day, change your agenda and go for a walk or sit in the sunshine. When you approach these fun activities with flexibility, you'll both enjoy yourselves more.

Don't Forget Yourself

Use these ideas to explore new hobbies and pursuits for yourself, too. Having fun and learning new things help you maintain your mental health and positive attitude. When your loved one is resting, devote some of that time to things you enjoy such as reading, exercising, or engaging in a hobby. There is no need to work all the time. You are a caregiver, not a slave or martyr. You deserve to spend time and energy on keeping your creativity and passions alive, too.

QUESTIONS FOR JOURNALING

What are you inspired to do to add more fun to your daily routine, both for yourself and your loved one?

What hobbies or interests might be enjoyable for your loved one?

How can you take advantage of the treasures in your hometown?

What do you think about asking your loved one to help you with chores?

Who else can help your loved one explore hobbies?

CHAPTER 19
Finances

When your loved one falls ill, your family finances are impacted. There will be extra expenses and most likely less income. You might need to stop working to become a full-time caregiver. You might need to apply for disability benefits for your loved one or wait for an insurance settlement. There will be co-pays, expenditures for medications and equipment, and lots of forms to complete. An AARP study called "Family Caregiving and Out-of-Pocket Costs: 2016 Report" estimated that family caregivers spent an average of $6,954 per year on out-of-pocket costs related to caregiving. (https://www.aarp.org/content/dam/aarp/research/surveys_statistics/ltc/2016/family-caregiving-costs-fact-sheet.doi.10.26419%252Fres.00138.002.pdf)

While you are focused primarily on your loved one's health, your finances can be a potential source of much stress as well. If you are caring for a parent, you might have to work with your siblings to ensure that everyone participates in financial decisions. If you are caring for a child, your spouse might disagree with some of your spending decisions. If you are caring for your spouse, you have to consider how you will cope with the loss of their income and the impact on your employment.

Many find financial conversations unpleasant and stressful. Money can bring out our worst, causing painful arguments and resentments. You've probably heard stories of families torn apart over selling the family home to pay medical expenses. Some families are financially devastated by medical costs and never recover. Money can cause lots of fear and worry, both for caregivers and loved ones.

One of the first things you can do to lessen financial stress is open a discussion with the appropriate parties. If you are caregiving for a child, you and the child's other parent will make financial decisions. If you are separated or divorced, consult your decrees to determine the non-custodial parent's responsibilities. If you are caring for your spouse, they should be part of financial discussions if they are able. When caring for a parent, you will involve siblings and their spouses. If your parent is divorced and remarried, you may have another layer of complication with a stepparent. Determine with whom you must discuss financial concerns.

Remember that unless your loved one is a child or has been declared incompetent, they are legally entitled to make their own financial decisions. This can be a challenging situation, especially after an illness that causes cognitive limitations such as dementia or stroke. If you need to take over your loved one's finances, you might need to consult with an attorney to determine how you can legally access accounts and manage money.

I believe strongly in working in partnership with Karen. We share financial information and work together to make decisions. It is respectful on my part and empowering for her to participate in financial decisions, and her right. If at all possible, invite your adult loved one to engage in ongoing financial discussions.

Once you have determined who needs to be involved in these discussions, use this list as a starting point for discussion:

- What assets and insurance coverages are available?
- Are there savings or IRAs that can be used to cover medical expenses?
- Does your loved one qualify for any local, state, or federal benefits, including veteran's benefits? If so, who can help with the application process?
- Which current recurring expenses must be paid and which can be comfortably eliminated if necessary?
- Who will be responsible for paying bills?
- Are there funds to reimburse caregiving expenses such as transportation, lodging, and supplies?
- Who will coordinate paperwork with insurance companies and other agencies?
- Are there funds for respite care?
- If your loved one cannot pay for their medical expenses, are other family members able and willing to contribute?
- What is the best place for your loved one to receive care at this time?

This final question has many layers. It could be that your loved one needs to go into long-term care, which is very costly. In some situations, a family member of someone who is eligible for Medicaid can be paid to provide care at home as an alternative under the In-Home Supportive Services program. (https://www.caregiver.org/what-every-caregiver-needs-know-about-money)

Depending on the situation, you may wish to consult your loved one's financial planner, attorney, and social worker. These professionals have experience navigating the complexities of financial management for someone with a severe illness. Social workers are experts in federal and state programs that assist those with serious illnesses. Some insurance companies assign a case manager or liaison. If your loved one needs costly medications, some drug companies have programs to help offset expenses.

Consider Tax Implications

Expenses for medical costs, transportation, respite care, and other caregiving expenses may be tax deductible. It is wise to keep an expense log and save receipts. Consult your tax preparer about the various deductions that might apply to your situation including:

- Claiming your loved one as a dependent
- The Child and Dependent Care Credit program
- Flexible spending accounts
- Itemized deductions related to your loved one's care including co-pays, therapy payments, and medical equipment expenses

(https://www.aarp.org/caregiving/financial-legal/info-2017/tax-tips-family-caregivers.html?intcmp=AE-CAR-LEG-EOA2)

Don't Forget You

It can be tempting to decline respite care and other needs for your well-being when money is tight. However, consider this: If you are no longer able to provide care for your loved one, who will?

In my opinion, investing in respite care, support groups, therapy, and other reasonable expenses to support your well-being is a wise use of money. It will cost much more to pay a professional caregiver than to invest a little in keeping you as healthy as possible. The Genworth Cost of Care Survey 2016 determined that in 2016 the cost of employing a home health aide full time for one year was nearly $46,480, and use of adult day services cost roughly $18,000. The same study found that the average annual cost for an assisted living facility was $43,539, and nursing home care was $92,378. (http://newsroom.genworth.com/2016-05-10-Genworth-2016-Annual-Cost-of-Care-Study-Costs-Continue-to-Rise-Particularly-for-Services-in-Home)

Your caregiving is worth a lot!

I have not been able to work outside my home for some time. Instead, I am Karen's full-time caregiver. There was a period when she was doing well, and I took a job. I had to leave it when the job required me to work unexpected extra shifts. There was also a strong chance that I could be injured or exposed to infections that could harm Karen. We decided that the risks were not worth the extra income.

Whether you can be employed and provide care is a question only you can answer. The answer may change over time depending on your loved one's medical status.

If you are working when your loved one becomes ill:

- Speak with your human resources personnel about Family Medical Leave Act support, which provides job protection and up to twelve weeks of unpaid and job-protected leave to care for family members with a serious illness. (https://www.dol.gov/whd/fmla)
- Discuss the situation with your supervisor and co-workers so they are not surprised if you must miss work for appointments and emergencies.
- Consider the financial impact on your future retirement if you stop working. Depending on your location, you may be required to purchase personal health insurance. Your future Social Security and pension payments will be impacted if you do not make any contributions for a period.

  https://www.caregiver.org/what-every-caregiver-needs-know-about-money

The Money Talk Never Ends

Financial discussions must be ongoing. If you are working with siblings, former spouses, or others, set up a way to keep everyone informed on a regular basis. Perhaps someone else would be willing to pay bills or manage communications so you can concentrate on caregiving. Ask for and accept any help you can get!

If you are caring for your spouse, work together to use your financial resources and plan for the future. Your loved one is probably just as worried as you are about money. They may feel guilty about the extra expenses. When you work in partnership, you'll ease their worries and enlist their help, which is very empowering.

Your loved one may be able to contribute by:

- Sorting and categorizing receipts
- Paying bills – online if that's easier for them
- Researching the best prices on things you need to purchase
- Shopping online for groceries, clothing, and other items. Home delivery is a time-saver and allows your loved one to make choices.

QUESTIONS FOR JOURNALING

Do you currently have any financial stressors related to caregiving?

Who can help you explore state and federal benefit programs?

Which family members might you be concerned about discussing financial matters with, and how can you solve the problem?

Finances

How do you feel about discussing finances with your loved one?

Do you feel more valuable now that you know your caregiving serves are worth nearly $50,000 each year?

CHAPTER 20
Intimacy and Romance

When you are providing care for your spouse, it is essential to keep the flames of intimacy and romance alive. Consider that when you began dating, you formed an alliance about how to express your affection for each other. When you were married, that alliance changed, and intimacy deepened as you began to live together on a full-time basis. Now that one of you has a medical condition, it is time to again negotiate your alliance in regard to intimacy.

The *Cambridge Dictionary* defines *intimacy* as "the state of having a close, personal relationship or a romantic relationship with someone." (https://dictionary.cambridge.org/dictionary/english/intimacy) So caregiving is certainly a very intimate act. You are providing personal care to your loved one and witnessing them in some of their most challenging moments. And yet, when you are caring for your spouse, the question of intimacy, romance, and sexual expression will occur to both of you. If you dare to address it in ongoing discussions, the two of you will be able to work together to find ways to be close that satisfy you both.

Things may be different than before, but can still be romantic and loving.

There are many ways to express intimacy. You can connect romantically by holding hands, lying side by side, cuddling, or laughing together. While you may not be able to go out dancing, you can listen to music together at home, perhaps even dancing a bit. You can light candles at dinnertime or create a special date night with take-out food.

Part of being an intentional caregiver is giving some thought to the intimate needs of both of you and creating a comfortable atmosphere for conversations about meeting those needs. Based on your relationship and comfort level, these conversations can be embarrassing at first. I suggest using a sense of humor, just as you do when you are assisting with bathing, toileting, and dressing. A sense of humor and the willingness to discuss intimacy gives you both the courage to address it regularly.

Intimacy is another area where your loved one can make choices. You can ask what kind of intimate or romantic expression would feel good, if any. There might be times when your partner feels very interested in intimacy and other times when they are too ill. Be sensitive to the fact that your loved one has lost privacy in the hospital. Many people have seen them naked. You and others may have assisted with toileting and dressing. There may be scars or body parts that don't work the way they used to. It can be hard to feel sexual or even attractive when you have been a patient for a long time. Intimacy and desire might wax and wane.

The Importance of Touch

Dr. Sharon K. Farber is a psychologist who studies the benefits of touch. She found that the act of touch during a massage, hug, or another version of physical touch releases physical and psychic pain from grief and loss. Touch stimulates the body to produce oxytocin, the hormone of love and attachment. (https://www.psychologytoday.com/us/blog/the-mind-body-connection/201309/why-we-all-need-touch-and-be-touched)

Physical contact can enhance the immune system, lower stress, and reduce anxiety. It can also create a feeling of safety, connection, and trust. (http://iheartintelligence.com/2017/03/07/human-touch) As a caregiver, you can provide the needed human connection by touching your loved one often. Hug, hold hands, apply lotion, brush hair, rub feet, massage, or sit close so your arms touch. Every loving touch helps your spouse feel connected and loved. Sometimes a loving touch says more than any words can.

Physical and Medical Limitations

Sexual expression is an important part of life for most people. Medical researcher William Burr writes in the *Canadian Medical Association Journal*, "The sexuality of people with disabilities, many of whom require varying degrees of assistance to lead fulfilling sex lives, continues to be overlooked, avoided or even dismissed as a component of holistic care because of a longstanding stigma that shrouds disability and sex." (CMAJ. 2011 Mar 22; 183(5): E259–E260. doi: 10.1503/cmaj.109-3813)

Your loved one might have physical limitations that impact sexual expression. Some people with heart problems, spinal cord injuries, or other medical conditions have challenges that preclude intercourse. It is important to discuss sexuality with a physician or nurse if you are concerned that intercourse might be harmful. It might be an embarrassing conversation, but your physician will have useful information, so it is wise to ask; and they've surely answered such questions before, so there's no need to be too embarrassed to ask.

There is also useful information online. You can search terms such as "sexuality after surgery," and "sexuality" plus the particular condition your loved one faces. You will be surprised how much information is available. There are even textbooks on the subject, many authored by physical therapists or physicians. Searching online resources together might be a comfortable way to find information. Like everything, if you can use a collaborative problem-solving approach with your loved one, the two of you will find ways to express your love physically that work for you.

You can begin your online searching with some of these sites:

- http://www.sexualityanddisability.org
- https://www.webmd.com/cancer/sex-after-cancer-treatment#1
- https://www.livestrong.org/we-can-help/finishing-treatment/male-sexual-health-after-cancer
- https://www.livestrong.org/we-can-help/finishing-treatment/female-sexual-health-after-cancer

Your loved one still has sexual needs even if they are ill or recovering. One of the first things you can do is remind your loved one that they are attractive and desirable. You can give compliments and make romantic gestures to demonstrate that you see them as more than their physical and medical challenges. Go slowly. You will know when it is the right time and place to discuss romance or even flirt a bit. Of course you won't have that kind of discussion right after surgery or during a medical crisis; trust your intuition and sense of timing.

When the time is right, talk about what might feel good, any pain or limitations, and how you might begin resuming a physical relationship if you both wish to. As always, approach these conversations as collaborations in which you both have ideas and suggestions. Over time you will find ways to foster intimacy and romance that both of you enjoy and cherish.

QUESTIONS FOR JOURNALING

How do you feel about discussing intimacy with your loved one?

Do you feel your loved one is well enough for intimacy? Have you discussed it with them?

What simple things can you do to demonstrate that you find your loved one attractive regardless of physical changes they're going through?

Can you arrange a date?

How often do you provide healing touch for your partner when not providing physical care?

Can you find ways to add more hand-holding, hugging, or other pleasurable touches to your daily routine?

CHAPTER 21
When Caregiving Ends

There will come a day when your caregiving tasks end. Your loved one will recover, pass away, or require placement in a care center. It's odd to think about it this way, but caregiving is a job with a definite ending. In one way or another, you are working yourself out of a job. You might provide care for days, weeks, or years, but at some point your caregiving service will be over.

When caregiving ends, you will likely feel a sense of confusion and lack of direction. For so long you've devoted yourself to your loved one. When they no longer require your full-time care, you may find yourself in limbo with too much time on your hands. These self-care ideas will help you navigate this time of transition intentionally and thoughtfully:

- **Recognize and remedy your exhaustion.** You will feel exhausted physically, mentally, emotionally, and spiritually. You've come through an intense situation that depleted you. Give yourself plenty of time to rest and restore your health with healthy foods and exercise.

If you find that you cannot sleep or have a poor appetite, and are not feeling a little better in a couple of weeks, see your physician for a checkup.

- **Avoid making crucial decisions right away.** Particularly after a death, you might have to make significant decisions about money, perhaps moving to a new home, and legal matters. Acknowledge that you need time to recover before making these decisions. It's your choice to wait until you feel ready to consider your situation.

- **Do things you have been putting off.** Take a trip, a course, or pick up a new hobby. Adding something new and enjoyable to your daily routine will help you have something to anticipate.

- **Give yourself time.** There is no timetable for caregiving recovery. You can't go buy a pair of new shoes, take a vacation, and expect that you'll be back to normal in a few days. Each person processes change differently. You might be tempted to return to work and bury yourself in business to avoid some of your pain. This would be a mistake. You deserve time and positive self-care.

- **Connect with others.** Caregiving may have required that you spent most of your time at home. Now purposely connect with friends and relatives to renew old relationships and make new ones. Consider hosting a small gathering at a local restaurant, seeing a play or concert, or making lunch dates with others. Isolation will make your recovery more challenging, so push yourself a bit to spend time with others.

- **Change your habits.** Your former routine centered

around your loved one, and you might feel as if no one needs you now that you are not providing full-time care. This is an ideal time to create healthy new routines. Consider volunteering, engaging in activities sponsored by your church or temple, joining a gym, or joining a community choral group. Anything that makes you happy and connects you with others is beneficial.

- **Process your emotions.** This is your most significant task. You will encounter feelings of relief, anger, sadness, loneliness, and guilt. The guilt will be particularly intense if your loved one is in a care center or has died. Your mind may torture you with guilt about things you did or did not do. It can seem as if you failed in your caregiving duties because your loved one did not recover. Because these feelings are so intense and troublesome, I highly recommend that you work with a therapist skilled in grief and loss recovery. A therapist can help you work through your emotions and has the training and experience to guide you towards recovery. There is a saying, "What you resist, persists." This is especially true with powerful emotions, which will fester and linger if you don't work through them. There will be things to forgive, both in you and in others. Let a therapist guide you through the process so you can recover your emotional balance.

- **Celebrate your accomplishments and memories.** Whether your loved one recovered or not, you kept your promise to them. You were a caregiver and lavished time, concern, and physical care to enable them to live at home. This is a worthy accomplishment! Find ways to honor yourself for that commitment. Dwell on the positive memories of your caregiving experience – the tenderness, the moments of connection, and the things you did in service to your loved one. You might want to create a ceremony, plant a tree, or donate in honor of your loved one. Find a meaningful way to recognize the gifts you gave each other.

- **Build a new identity over time.** It is easy to wrap your identity into that of your loved one. When they have a good day, so do you. When they have a setback, you experience it, too. Now that you are no longer a full-time caregiver, you need a new role. What will you become next?

- **If your loved one has entered a care facility:** You might struggle with how much time to spend there. You might feel guilty if you are not there every day or even every hour. Do your best to find a healthy balance between trusting the care facility to provide the physical care for your loved one, spending enough time there to oversee care and connect with them, and taking time for yourself. There is no formula for this, as each situation is different. Find a combination that works for both of you.

As you can see, the end of caregiving is a time of profound healing and transition. Be kind to yourself. You will find new ways to use your time, connect with others, and explore new roles. Don't be alarmed if it takes more time than you anticipated or you feel you are taking one step forward and three steps back. Honor your process and recognize that it will be a spiral path instead of straight line. You can do it!

QUESTIONS FOR JOURNALING

Describe a possible future in which you are no longer providing care. What would you do with your extra time and energy?

Do you fear the end of caregiving? What can you do to resolve your fear?

Do you know others who can share their post-caregiving experiences with you?

How do you feel about joining a caregiving support group?

How can you capture and preserve positive memories now?

CHAPTER 22
Finding and Maintaining Joy

Karen has a tracheotomy. On rare occasions she has seizures and I need to use an Ambu bag to breathe for her until the ambulance arrives. This bag is like a football that I pump with my hand to send air into her lungs. I've only had to use it twice since she had the tracheotomy. Both times I was terrified. She was turning blue. Her life was literally in my hands, dependent on my properly following the training I'd received on how to use the bag. I remember the first time when the paramedics arrived; I must have looked awful because they thought I was the patient and having a heart attack.

As a caregiver, you will encounter situations about which you are frightened, and you might feel overwhelmed by the responsibility you have for your loved one's life. In those moments, the only thing you can do is trust yourself and your training. When the crisis has abated, you'll experience intense emotions. This is a typical reaction – you are not going crazy!

It is beneficial to have established a relationship with a therapist, coach, or support group before such a situation arises so you can get immediate help processing your emotions if that happens. One thing you will realize is that it is terribly uncomfortable to come face to face with your helplessness. You can do everything possible for your loved one except control their medical situation.

My mother's care team offered no hope for her recovery after her stroke. Later, when she was diagnosed with cancer, I felt even more helpless because I could not save her. I had to make a distinction between my areas of control and those I had to leave up to the Universe. I could not cure her, but I could make sure that her quality of life was as positive as it could be in her situation.

We are brought up to measure ourselves against outcomes. We study for a test and get a grade. We go to a job interview and hope to be selected for the position. We exercise and see that we have more stamina or can wear smaller jeans. In much of life, our efforts produce an outcome. Caregiving does not work that way. You can be the best caregiver in the world, do everything correctly, and your loved one may not recover. You need a different measure of success.

This understanding is crucial for your mental health as a caregiver. You are not in charge of any outcomes, cures, or recovery. It's a hard truth because you want to be able to take away pain and sickness from the person you love so much. But you are only in charge of your loved one's quality of life – and that is a sacred responsibility.

Once you embrace that distinction, you will be able to approach caregiving in a more empowered way. You will notice and treasure the small, tender moments when you eased your loved one's stress, held their hand, helped them complete a task that was meaningful to them, or made them laugh. These moments of quiet joy are your reward. You will treasure them always.

I feel lucky that I got to spend time with my mother at the end of her life. I remember just being with her, watching movies, telling stories, and hearing her laugh. The feel of her hand in mine still lingers. In those moments, everything else fell away. I did not worry about the logistics of her care, her life expectancy, or when I was going to do the laundry. I felt joy just being with her, and a sense of peace that came from knowing I was doing my best to give her a positive quality of life. Many people never get to experience those extraordinary moments. I've been blessed to have lots of them, both with my mother and with Karen.

When Karen and I go for a drive and have ice cream, we're happy. Everything is right at that moment, and we don't need anything else. I've had the honor of being beside her in moments of great pain and of great triumph. She's been beside me in similar moments, seeing me at my best and my worst. And we still love each other. Those moments of joy and connection are more precious to me than anything else in the world.

In the final analysis, your role as an intentional caregiver boils down to just a few things:

- Doing the very best you can to enhance your loved one's quality of life
- Keeping yourself healthy mentally, physically, and emotionally
- Noticing and cherishing all the moments of joy

Whatever situation you and your loved one face, whether there is hope for recovery or not, your caregiving makes a profound difference. Trust yourself, get support, and watch for moments of joy. They will often surprise you. Moments of laughter, peace, and connection are available in every caregiving situation, regardless of your loved one's medical condition.

I wish you strength, courage, support, and many beautiful moments of joy in your caregiving journey.

About the Author

Geoffrey Grant earned a B.A. in Communications from Curry College in Milton, Massachusetts. He's been a full-time caregiver for twenty years.

Geoffrey provides support, coaching, and workshops for other caregivers, both in person and virtually. He also does presentations on caregiving in hospitals, community centers, and the media.

For more information and resources for caregivers, visit GeoffGrantConsulting.com

Acknowledgments

Many people supported my care-giving journey with love, support, encouragement and friendship. I thank you all.

There are a few people who made extraordinary contributions: The late Dr. David J. Sugarbaker, Roger and Lois Chadwick, Roger Chadwick Jr. and family, Kevin Chadwick and family, and Alex Grant and family. To all the staff at Brigham and Women's Hospital and Dana Farber Cancer Institute, a million thank yous

www.ingramcontent.com/pod-product-compliance
Lightning Source LLC
Chambersburg PA
CBHW071452040426
42444CB00008B/1305